The Children's Blue Bird

The Children's Blue Bird

By

Georgette Leblanc

Translated by

Alexander Teixeira De Mattos

New York
Dodd, Mead and Company
1967

PRINTED IN THE UNITED STATES OF AMERICA

Contents

The Woodcutter's Cottage

CHAPTER I

THE WOODCUTTER'S COTTAGE

ONCE upon a time, a woodcutter and his wife lived in their cottage on the edge of a large and ancient forest. They had two dear little children who met with a most wonderful adventure.

But, before telling you all about it, I must describe the children to you and let you know something of their character; for, if they had not been so sweet and brave and plucky, the curious story which you are about to hear would never have happened at all.

Tyltyl—that was our hero's name—was ten years old; and Mytyl, his little sister, was only six.

Tyltyl was a fine, tall little fellow, stout and well-set-up, with curly black hair which was often in a tangle, for he was fond of a romp. He was a great favourite because of his smiling and good-tempered face and the bright look in his eyes; but, best of all, he had the ways of a bold and fearless little man, which showed the noble qualities of his heart. When, early in the morning, he trotted along the

3

forest-road by the side of his daddy, Tyl the woodcutter, for all his shabby clothes he looked so proud and gallant that every beautiful thing on the earth and in the sky seemed to lie in wait for him to smile upon him as he passed.

His little sister was very different, but looked ever so sweet and pretty in her long frock, which Mummy Tyl kept neatly patched for her. She was as fair as her brother was dark; and her large timid eyes were blue as the forget-me-nots in the fields. Anything was enough to frighten her and she would cry at the least thing; but her little child's soul already held the highest womanly qualities: she was loving and gentle and so fondly devoted to her brother that, rather than abandon him, she did not hesitate to undertake a long and dangerous journey in his company.

What happened and how our little hero and heroine went off into the world one night in search of happiness: that is the subject of my story.

Daddy Tyl's cottage was the poorest of the countryside; and it seemed even more wretched because it stood opposite a splendid hall in which rich children lived. From the windows of the cottage you could see what went on inside the Hall when the dining-room and drawing-rooms were lit up in the evening. And, in the daytime, you saw the little children playing on the terraces, in the gardens and in the hot-houses which people came all the way from town to visit because they were always filled with the rarest flowers.

Now, one evening which was not like other evenings, for it was Christmas Eve, Mummy Tyl put her little ones to bed and kissed them even more lovingly than usual. She felt a little sad, because owing to the stormy weather, Daddy Tyl was not able to go to work in the forest; and so she had no money to buy presents with which to fill Tyltyl and Mytyl's stockings. The Children soon fell asleep, everything was still and silent and not a sound was heard but the purring of the cat, the snoring of the dog and the ticking of the great grandfather's clock. But suddenly a light as bright as day crept through the shutters, the lamp upon the table lit again of itself and the two Children awoke, yawned, rubbed their eyes, stretched out their arms in bed and Tyltyl, in a cautious voice called:

"Mytyl?"

"Yes, Tyltyl?" was the answer.

"Are you asleep?"

"Are you?"

"No," said Tyltyl. "How can I be asleep, when I'm talking to you?"

"I say, is this Christmas Day?" asked his sister.

"Not yet; not till to-morrow. But Father Christmas won't bring us anything this year."

"Why not?"

"I heard Mummy say that she couldn't go to town to tell him. But he will come next year."

"Is next year far off?"

"A good long while," said the boy. "But he will come to the rich children to-night."

"Really?"

"Hullo!" cried Tyltyl of a sudden. "Mummy's forgotten to put out the lamp! . . . I've an idea!"

"What?"

"Let's get up."

"But we mustn't," said Mytyl, who always remembered.

"Why, there's no one about! . . . Do you see the shutters?"

"Oh, how bright they are!" . . .

"It's the lights of the party," said Tyltyl.

"What party?"

"The rich children opposite. It's the Christmas-tree. Let's open the shutters. . . ."

"Can we?" asked Mytyl, timidly.

"Of course we can; there's no one to stop us. . . . Do you hear the music? . . . Let us get up."

The two Children jumped out of bed, ran to the window, climbed on the stool in front of it and threw back the shutters. A bright light filled the room; and the Children looked out eagerly:

"We can see everything!" said Tyltyl.

"I can't," said poor little Mytyl, who could hardly find room on the stool.

"It's snowing!" said Tyltyl. "There's two carriages, with six horses each!"

"There are twelve little boys getting out!" said Mytyl, who was doing her best to peep out of the window.

"Don't be silly! . . . They're little girls . . ."

"They've got knickerbockers on . . ."

"Do be quiet! . . . And look! . . ."

"What are those gold things there, hanging from the branches?"

"Why, toys, to be sure!" said Tyltyl. "Swords, guns, soldiers, cannons. . . ."

"And what's that, all round the table?"

"Cakes and fruit and cream-tarts."

"Oh, how pretty the children are!" cried Mytyl, clapping her hands.

"And how they're laughing and laughing!" answered Tyltyl, rapturously.

"And the little ones dancing! . . ."

"Yes, yes; let's dance too!" shouted Tyltyl.

And the two Children began to stamp their feet for joy on the stool:

"Oh, what fun!" said Mytyl.

"They're getting the cakes!" cried Tyltyl. "They can touch them! . . . They're eating, they're eating, they're eating! . . . Oh, how lovely, how lovely! . . ."

Mytyl began to count imaginary cakes:

"I have twelve! . . ."

"And I four times twelve!" said Tyltyl. "But I'll give you some. . . ."

And our little friends, dancing, laughing and shrieking with delight, rejoiced so prettily in the other children's happiness that they forgot their own poverty and want. They were soon to have their reward. Suddenly, there came a loud knocking at the door. The startled Children ceased their romp and dared not move a limb. Then the big wooden latch lifted of itself, with a loud creak; the door opened slowly: and in crept a little old woman, dressed all in green, with a red hood over her head. She was hump-backed and lame and had only one eye; her nose and chin almost touched; and she walked leaning on a stick. She was obviously a fairy.

She hobbled up to the Children and asked, in a snuffling voice:

"Have you the grass here that sings or the bird that is blue?"

"We have some grass," replied Tyltyl, trembling all over his body, "but it can't sing . . ."

"Tyltyl has a bird," said Mytyl.

"But I can't give it away, because it's mine," the little fellow added, quickly.

Now wasn't that a capital reason?

The Fairy put on her big, round glasses and looked at the bird:

"He's not blue enough," she exclaimed. "I must absolutely have the Blue Bird. It's for my little girl, who is very ill . . . Do you know what the Blue Bird stands for? No? I thought you didn't; and, as you are good children, I will tell you."

The Fairy raised her crooked finger to her long, pointed nose, and whispered, in a mysterious tone:

"The Blue Bird stands for happiness; and I want you

to understand that my little girl must be happy in order to get well. That is why I now command you to go out into the world and find the Blue Bird for her. You will have to start at once . . . Do you know who I am?"

The Children exchanged puzzled glances. The fact was that they had never seen a fairy before; and they felt a little scared in her presence. However, Tyltyl soon said politely:

"You are rather like our neighbour, Madame Berlingot . . ."

Tyltyl thought that, in saying this, he was paying the Fairy a compliment; for Madame Berlingot's shop, which was next door to their cottage, was a very pleasant place. It was stocked with sweets, marbles, chocolate cigars and sugar cocks-and-hens; and, at fair-time, there were big gingerbread dolls covered all over with gilt paper. Goody Berlingot had a nose that was quite as ugly as the Fairy's; she was old also; and, like the Fairy, she walked doubled up in two; but she was very kind and she had a dear little girl who used to play on Sundays with the woodcutter's Children. Unfortunately, the poor little pretty, fair-haired thing was always suffering from some unknown complaint, which often kept her in bed. When this happened, she used to beg and pray for Tyltyl's dove to play with; but Tyltyl was so fond of the bird that he would not give it to her. All this, thought the little boy, was very like that what the Fairy told him; and that was why he called her Berlingot.

Much to his surprise, the Fairy turned crimson with rage. It was a hobby of hers to be like nobody, because she was a fairy and able to change her appearance, from one moment to the next, as she pleased. That evening, she happened to be ugly and old and hump-backed; she had lost one of her eyes; and two lean wisps of grey hair hung over her shoulders.

"What do I look like?" she asked Tyltyl. "Am I pretty or ugly? Old or young?"

Her reason for asking these questions was to try the kindness of the little boy. He turned away his head and dared not say what he thought of her looks. Then she cried:

"I am the Fairy Bérylune!"

"Oh, that's all right!" answered Tyltyl, who, by this time, was shaking in every limb.

This mollified the Fairy; and, as the Children were still in their night-shirts, she told them to get dressed. She herself helped Mytyl and, while she did so, asked:

"Where are your Father and Mother?"

"In there," said Tyltyl, pointing to the door on the right. "They're asleep."

"And your Grandad and Granny?"

"They're dead. . . ."

"And your little brothers and sisters . . . Have you any? . . ."

"Oh, yes, three little brothers!" said Tyltyl.

"And four little sisters," added Mytyl.

"Where are they?" asked the Fairy.

"They are dead, too," answered Tyltyl.

"Would you like to see them again?"

"Oh, yes! . . . At once! . . . Show them to us! . . . "

"I haven't got them in my pocket," said the Fairy. "But this is very lucky; you will see them when you go through the Land of Memory. It's on the way to the Blue Bird, just on the left, past the third turning . . . What were you doing when I knocked?"

"We were playing at eating cakes," said Tyltyl.

"Have you any cakes? . . . Where are they? . . ."

"In the house of the rich children . . . Come and look, it's so lovely!"

And Tyltyl dragged the Fairy to the window.

"But it's the others who are eating them!" said she.

"Yes, but we can see them eat," said Tyltyl.

"Aren't you cross with them?"

"What for?"

"For eating all the cakes. I think it's very wrong of them not to give you any."

"Not at all; they're rich! . . . I say, isn't it beautiful over there?"

"It's just the same here, only you can't see. . . ."

"Yes, I can," said Tyltyl. "I have very good eyes. I can see the time on the church clock; and Daddy can't!"

The Fairy suddenly grew angry:

"I tell you that you can't see!" she said.

And she grew angrier and angrier. As though it mattered about seeing the time on the church clock!

Of course, the little boy was not blind; but, as he was kind-hearted and deserved to be happy, she wanted to teach him to see what is good and beautiful in all things. It was not an easy task, for she well knew that most people live and die without enjoying the happiness that lies all around them. Still, as she was a fairy, she was all-powerful; and so she decided to give him a little hat adorned with a magic diamond that would possess the extraordinary property of always showing him the truth, which would help him to see the inside of Things and thus teach him that each of them has a life and an existence of its own, created to match and gladden ours.

The Fairy took the little hat from a great bag hanging by her side. It was green and had a white cockade, with the big diamond shining in the middle of it. Tyltyl was beside himself with delight. The Fairy explained to him how the diamond worked. By pressing the top, you saw the soul of Things; if you gave it a little turn to the right, you discovered the Past; and, when you turned it to the left, you beheld the Future.

Tyltyl beamed all over his face and danced for joy; and then he at once became afraid of losing the little hat:

"Daddy will take it from me!" he cried.

"No," said the Fairy, "for no one can see it as long as it's on your head . . . Will you try it?"

"Yes, yes!" cried the Children, clapping their hands.

The hat was no sooner on the little boy's head than a magic change came over everything. The old Fairy turned into a young and beautiful princess, dressed all in silk and covered with sparkling jewels; the walls of the cottage became transparent and gleamed like precious stones; the humble deal furniture shone like marble. The two children ran from right to left clapping their hands and shouting with delight.

"Oh, how lovely, how lovely!" exclaimed Tyltyl.

And Mytyl, like the vain little thing she was, stood spell-bound before the beauty of the fair princess' dress.

But further and much greater surprises were in store for them. Had not the Fairy said that the Things and the Animals would come to life, talk and behave like every-body else? Lo and behold, suddenly the door of the grand-father's clock opened, the silence was filled with the sweetest music and twelve little daintily-dressed and laughing dancers began to skip and spin all around the Children.

"They are the Hours of your life," said the Fairy.

"May I dance with them?" asked Tyltyl, gazing with admiration at those pretty creatures, who seemed to skim over the floor like birds.

But just then he burst into a wild fit of laughter! Who was that funny fat fellow, all out of breath and covered with flour, who came struggling out of the bread-pan and bowing to the children? It was Bread! Bread himself, taking advantage of the reign of liberty to go for a little walk on earth! He looked like a stout, comical old gen-tleman; his face was puffed out with dough; and his large hands, at the end of his thick arms, were not able to meet, when he laid them on his great, round stomach. He was dressed in a tight-fitting crust-coloured suit, with stripes across the chest like those on the nice buttered rolls which we have for breakfast in the morning. On his head—just think of it!—he wore an enormous bun, which made a funny sort of turban.

He had hardly tumbled out of his pan, when other loaves just like him, but smaller, followed after and began to frisk about with the Hours, without giving a thought to the flour which they scattered over those pretty ladies and which wrapped them in great white clouds.

It was a queer and charming dance; and the Children were delighted. The Hours waltzed with the loaves; the plates, joining in the fun, hopped up and down on the dresser, at the risk of falling off and smashing to pieces; the glasses in the cupboard clinked together, to drink the health of one and all. As to the forks, they chattered so loudly with the knives that you could not hear yourself speak for the noise. . . .

There is no knowing what would have happened if the din had lasted much longer. Daddy and Mummy Tyl would certainly have woke up. Fortunately, when the romp was at its height, an enormous flame darted out of the chimney and filled the room with a great red glow, as though the house were on fire. Everybody bolted into the corners in dismay, while Tyltyl and Mytyl, sobbing with fright, hid their heads under the good Fairy's cloak.

"Don't be afraid," she said. "It's only Fire, who has come to join in your fun. He is a good sort, but you had better not touch him, for he has a nasty temper."

Peeping anxiously through the beautiful gold lace that edged the Fairy's cloak, the Children saw a tall, red fellow looking at them and laughing at their fears. He was dressed in scarlet tights and spangles; from his shoulders hung silk scarves that were just like flames when he waved them with his long arms; and his hair stood up on his head in straight, flaring locks. He started flinging out his arms and legs and jumping round the room like a madman.

Tyltyl, though feeling a little easier, dared not yet leave his refuge. Then the Fairy Bérylune had a capital idea: she pointed her wand at the tap; and at once there appeared a young girl who wept like a regular fountain. It was Water. She was very pretty, but she looked extremely sad; and she sang so sweetly that it was like the rippling of a spring. Her long hair, which fell to her feet, might have been made of sea-weed. She had nothing on but her bed-gown; but the water that streamed over her clothed her in shimmering colours. She hesitated at first and gave a glance around her; then, catching sight of Fire still whirling about like a great madcap, she made an angry and indignant rush at him, spraying his face, splashing and wetting him with all her might. Fire flew into a rage and began to smoke. Nevertheless, as he found himself suddenly thwarted by his hereditary enemy, he thought it wiser to retire to a corner. Water also beat a retreat; and it seemed as though peace would be restored once more.

The two Children, at last recovering from their alarm, were asking the Fairy what was going to happen next, when a startling noise of breaking crockery made them look round towards the table. What a surprise! The milk-jug lay on the floor, smashed into a thousand fragments, and from the pieces rose a charming lady, who gave little screams of terror and clasped her hands and turned up her eyes with a beseeching glance.

Tyltyl hastened to console her, for he at once knew that she was Milk; and, as he was very fond of her, he gave her a good kiss. She was as fresh and pretty as a little dairy-maid; and a delicious scent of hay came from her white frock all covered with cream.

Meanwhile, Mytyl was watching the sugar-loaf, which also seemed to be coming to life. Packed in its blue paper wrapper, on a shelf near the door, it was swaying from left to right and from right to left without any result. But at

last a long thin arm was seen to come out, followed by a
peaked head, which split the paper, and by another arm and
two long legs that seemed never to end! . . . Oh, you
should have seen how funny Sugar looked: so funny, indeed, that the Children could not help laughing in his face!
And yet they would have liked to be civil to him, for they
heard the Fairy introducing him in these words:

"This, Tyltyl, is the soul of Sugar. His pockets are
crammed with sugar and each of his fingers is a sugar-
stick."

How wonderful to have a friend all made of sugar, off
whom you can bite a piece whenever you feel inclined!

"Bow, wow, wow! . . . Good-morning! Good-morning,
my little god! . . . At last, at last we can talk! . . . Bark
and wag my tail as I might, you never understood! . . . I
love you! I love you!"

Who can this extraordinary person be, who jostles everybody and fills the house with his noisy gaiety? We know
him at once. It is Tylô, the good Dog who tries his hardest
to understand mankind, the good-natured Animal who
goes with the Children to the forest, the faithful guardian
who protects the door, the staunch friend who is ever true
and ever loyal! Here he comes walking on his hind-
paws, as on a pair of legs too short for him, and

beating the air with the two others, making gestures like a clumsy little man. He has not changed: he still has his smooth, mustard-coloured coat and his jolly bull-dog head, with the black muzzle, but he is much bigger and then he talks! He talks as fast as he can, as though he wanted in one moment to avenge his whole race, which has been doomed to silence for centuries. He talks of everything, now that he is at last able to unbosom himself; and it is a pretty sight to see him kissing his little master and mistress and calling them "his little gods!" He sits up, he jumps about the room, knocking against the furniture, upsetting Mytyl with his big soft paws, lolling his tongue, wagging his tail and puffing and panting as though he were out hunting. We at once see his simple, generous nature. Persuaded of his own importance, he fancies that he alone is indispensable in the new world of Things.

After making all the fuss he wanted of the Children, he started going the round of the company, distributing the attentions which he thought that none could do without. His joy, now set free, found vent without restraint; and, because he was the most loving of creatures, he would also have been the happiest, if, in becoming human, he had not, unfortunately, retained his little doggy failings. He was jealous! He was terribly jealous; and his heart felt a pang when he saw Tylette, the Cat, coming to life in her turn and being petted and kissed by the Children, just as he had been! Oh, how he hated the Cat! To bear the sight of her beside him, to see her always sharing in the affection of the family: that was the great sacrifice which fate demanded of him. He accepted it, however, without a word, because it pleased his little gods; and he went so far as to leave her alone. But he had had many a crime on his conscience because of her! Had he not, one evening, crept stealthily into Goody Berlingot's kitchen in order to throttle her old tom-cat, who had never done him any harm? Had he not broken the back of the Persian cat at the Hall opposite? Did he not sometimes go to town on purpose to hunt cats and put an end to them, all to wreak his spite? And now Tylette was going to talk, just like himself! Tylette would be his equal in the new world that was opening before him!

"Oh, there is no justice left on earth!" was his bitter thought. "There is no justice left!"

In the meantime, the Cat, who had begun by washing herself and polishing her claws, calmly put out her paw to the little girl.

She really was a very pretty cat; and, if our friend Tylô's jealousy had not been such an ugly feeling, we might almost have overlooked it for once! How could you fail to be attracted by Tylette's eyes, which were like topaz set in emeralds? How could you resist the pleasure of stroking the wonderful black velvet back? How could you not love her grace, her gentleness and the dignity of her poses?

Smiling amiably and speaking in well-chosen language, she said to Mytyl:

"Good-morning, miss! . . . How well you look this morning! . . ."

And the Children patted her like anything.

Tylô kept watching the Cat from the other end of the room:

"Now that she's standing on her hind-legs like a man," he muttered, "she looks just like the Devil, with her pointed ears, her long tail and her dress as black as ink!" And he could not help growling between his teeth. "She's also like the village chimney-sweep," he went on, "whom I loathe and detest and whom I shall never take for a real man, whatever my little gods may say . . . It's lucky," he added, with a sigh, "that I know more about a good many things than they do!"

But suddenly, no longer able to master himself, he flew at the Cat and shouted, with a loud laugh that was more like a roar:

"I'm going to frighten Tylette! Bow, wow, wow!"

But the Cat, who was dignified even when still an animal, now thought herself called to the loftiest destinies. She considered that the time had come to raise an insuperable barrier between herself and the Dog, who had never been more than an ill-bred person in her eyes; and, stepping back in disdain, she just said:

"Sir, I don't know you."

Tylô gave a bound under the insult, whereupon the Cat bristled up, twisting her whiskers under her little pink nose (for she was very proud of those two pale blotches which gave a special touch to her dark beauty) ; and then, arching her back and sticking up her tail, she hissed out, "Fft! Fft!" and stood stock-still on the chest of drawers, like a dragon on the lid of a Chinese vase.

Tyltyl and Mytyl screamed with laughter; but the quarrel would certainly have had a bad ending if, at that moment, a great thing had not happened. At eleven o'clock in the evening, in the middle of that winter's night, a great light, the light of the noon-day sun, glowing and dazzling, burst into the cottage.

"Hullo, there's daylight!" said the little boy, who no longer knew what to make of things. "What will Daddy say?"

But, before the Fairy had time to set him right, Tyltyl

understood; and, full of wonderment, he knelt before the latest apparition that bewitched his eyes.

At the window, in the centre of a great halo of sunshine, there rose slowly, like a tall golden sheaf, a maiden of surpassing loveliness! Gleaming veils covered her figure without hiding its beauty; her bare arms, stretched in the attitude of giving, seemed transparent; and her great clear eyes wrapped all upon whom they fell in a fond embrace.

"It's the Queen!" said Tyltyl.

"It's the Blessed Virgin!" cried Mytyl, kneeling beside her brother.

"No, my Children," said the Fairy. "It is Light!"

Smiling, Light stepped towards the two little ones. She, the Light of Heaven, the strength and beauty of the Earth, was proud of the humble mission entrusted to her; she, never before held captive, living in space and lavishing her bounty upon all alike, consented to be confined, for a brief spell, within a human shape, so as to lead the Children out into the world and teach them to know that other Light, the Light of the Mind, which we never see, but which helps us to see all things that are.

"It is Light!" exclaimed the Things and the Animals; and, as they all loved her, they began to dance around her with cries of pleasure.

Tyltyl and Mytyl capered with joy. Never had they pictured so amusing and so pretty a party; and they shouted louder than all the rest.

Then what was bound to happen came. Suddenly, three knocks were heard against the wall, loud enough to throw the house down! It was Daddy Tyl, who had been woke up by the din and who was now threatening to come and put a stop to it.

"Turn the diamond!" cried the Fairy to Tyltyl.

Our hero hastened to obey, but he had not the knack of it yet; besides, his hand shook at the thought that his father was coming. In fact, he was so awkward that he nearly broke the works.

"Not so quick, not so quick!" said the Fairy. "Oh dear, you've turned it too briskly: they will not have time to resume their places and we shall have a lot of bother!"

There was a general stampede. The walls of the cottage lost their splendour. All ran hither and thither, to return to their proper shape: Fire could not find his chimney; Water ran about looking for her tap; Sugar stood moaning in front of his torn wrapper; and Bread, the biggest of the loaves, was unable to squeeze into his pan, in which the other loaves had jumped higgledy-piggledy, taking up all the room. As for the Dog, he had grown too large for the hole in his kennel; and the Cat also could not get into her basket. The Hours alone, who were accustomed always to run faster than Man wished, had slipped back into the clock without delay.

Light stood motionless and unruffled, vainly setting an example of calmness to the others, who were all weeping and wailing around the Fairy:

"What is going to happen?" they asked. "Is there any danger?"

"Well," said the Fairy, "I am bound to tell you the truth: all those who accompany the two Children will die at the end of the journey."

They began to cry like anything, all except the Dog, who was delighted at remaining human as long as possible and who had already taken his stand next to Light, so as to be sure of going in front of his little master and mistress.

At that moment, there came a knocking even more dreadful than before.

"There's Daddy again!" said Tyltyl. "He's getting up, this time; I can hear him walking . . ."

"You see," said the Fairy, "you have no choice now; it is too late; you must all start with us . . . But you, Fire, don't come near anybody; you, Dog, don't tease the Cat; you, Water, try not to run all over the place; and you, Sugar,

stop crying, unless you want to melt. Bread shall carry
the cage in which to put the Blue Bird; and you shall all
come to my house, where I will dress the Animals and the
Things properly . . . Let us go out this way!"

As she spoke, she pointed her wand at the window, which
lengthened magically downwards, like a door. They all
went out on tip-toe, after which the window resumed its
usual shape. And so it came about that, on Christmas
Night, in the clear light of the moon, while the bells rang
out lustily, proclaiming the birth of Jesus, Tyltyl and
Mytyl went in search of the Blue Bird that was to bring
them happiness.

At the Fairy's

CHAPTER II

AT THE FAIRY'S

THE Fairy Bérylune's Palace stood at the top of a very high mountain, on the way to the moon. It was so near that, on summer nights, when the sky was clear, you could plainly see the moon's mountains and valleys, lakes and seas from the terrace of the palace. Here the Fairy studied the stars and read their secrets, for it was long since the Earth had had anything to teach her.

"This old planet no longer interests me!" she used to say to her friends, the giants of the mountain. "The men upon it still live with their eyes shut! Poor things, I pity them! I go down among them now and then, but it is out of charity, to try and save the little children from the fatal misfortune that awaits them in the darkness."

This explains why she had come and knocked at the door of Daddy Tyl's cottage on Christmas Eve.

And now to return to our travellers. They had hardly reached the high-road, when the Fairy remembered that they could not walk like that through the village, which was still lit up because of the feast.   But her store of knowledge was so great that all her wishes were fulfilled at once.   She pressed lightly on Tyltyl's head and willed that they should all be carried by magic to her palace.   Then and there, a cloud of fireflies surrounded our companions and wafted them gently towards the sky.   They were at the Fairy's palace before they had recovered from their surprise.

"Follow me," she said and led them through chambers and passages all in gold and silver.

They stopped in a large room surrounded with mirrors on every side and containing an enormous wardrobe with light creeping through its chinks.   The Fairy Bérylune took a diamond key from her pocket and opened the wardrobe. One cry of amazement burst from every throat.   Precious stuffs were seen piled one on the top of the other: mantles covered with gems, dresses of every sort and every country, pearl coronets, emerald necklaces, ruby bracelets . . . Never had the Children beheld such riches!   As for the Things, their state was rather one of utter bewilderment; and this was only natural, when you think that they were seeing the world for the first time and that it showed itself to them in such a queer way.

The Fairy helped them make their choice.   Fire, Sugar and the Cat displayed a certain decision of taste.   Fire, who

only cared for red, at once chose a splendid Mephistopheles
dress, with gold spangles. He put nothing on his head, for
his head was always very hot. Sugar could not stand anything except white and pale blue: bright colours jarred on
his sweet nature. The long blue and white dress which he
selected and the pointed hat, like a candle extinguisher,
which he wore on his head made him look perfectly ridiculous; but he was too silly to notice it and kept spinning before the glass like a top and admiring himself in blissful
ignorance.

The Cat, who was always a lady and who was used to her
dusky garments, reflected that black always looks well, in
any circumstance, particularly now, when they were travel-
ling without luggage. She therefore put on a suit of black
tights, with jet embroidery, hung a long velvet cloak from
her shoulders and perched a large cavalier hat, with a long
feather, on her neat little head. She next asked for a pair
of soft kid boots, in memory of Puss-in-Boots, her distin-
guished ancestor, and put a pair of gloves on her fore-paws,
to protect them from the dust of the roads.

Thus attired, she took a satisfied glance at the mirror.
Then, a little nervously, with an anxious eye and a quivering pink nose, she hastily invited Sugar and Fire to take the
air with her. So they all three walked out, while the others

went on dressing. Let us follow them for a moment, for
we have already grown to like our brave little Tyltyl and
we shall want to hear anything that is likely to help or delay
his undertaking.

After passing through several splendid galleries, hung
like balconies in the sky, our three cronies stopped in the
hall; and the Cat at once addressed the meeting in a hushed
voice:

"I have brought you here," she said, "in order to discuss
the position in which we are placed. Let us make the most
of our last moment of liberty . . ."

But she was interrupted by a furious uproar:

"Bow, wow, wow!"

"There now!" cried the Cat. "There's that idiot of a
Dog! He has scented us out! We can't get a minute's
peace. Let us hide behind the balustrade. He had better
not hear what I have to say to you."

"It's too late," said Sugar, who was standing by the door.

And, sure enough, Tylô was coming up, jumping, barking,
panting and delighted.

The Cat, when she saw him, turned away in disgust:

"He has put on the livery of one of the footmen of Cinder-
ella's coach . . . It is just the thing for him: he has the soul
of a flunkey!"

She ended these words with a "Fft! Fft!" and, stroking her whiskers, took up her stand, with a defiant air, between Sugar and Fire. The good Dog did not see her little game. He was wholly wrapped up in the pleasure of being gorgeously arrayed; and he danced round and round. It was really funny to see his velvet coat whirling like a merry-go-round, with the skirts opening every now and then and showing his little stumpy tail, which was all the more expressive as it had to express itself very briefly. For I need hardly tell you that Tylô, like every well-bred bull-dog, had had his tail and his ears cropped as a puppy.

Poor fellow, he had long envied the tails of his brother dogs, which allowed them to use a much larger and more varied vocabulary. But physical deficiencies and the hardships of fortune strengthen our innermost qualities. Tylô's soul, having no outward means of unbosoming itself, had only gained through silence; and his look, which was always filled with love, had become tremendously eloquent.

To-day his big dark eyes glistened with delight; he had suddenly changed into a man! He was all over magnificent clothes; and he was about to perform a grand errand across the world in company with the gods!

"There!" he said. "There! Aren't we fine! . . . Just

look at this lace and embroidery! . . . It's real gold and no
mistake!"

He did not see that the others were laughing at him, for,
to tell the truth, he did look very comical; but, like all simple creatures, he had no sense of humour. He was so proud
of his natural garment of yellow hair that he had put on
no waistcoat, in order that no one might have a doubt as to
where he sprang from. For the same reason, he had kept his
collar, with his address on it. A big red velvet coat, heavily
braided with gold-lace, reached to his knees; and the large
pockets on either side would enable him, he thought, always
to carry a few provisions; for Tylô was very greedy. On his
left ear, he wore a little round cap with an osprey-feather
in it and he kept it on his big square head by means of an
elastic which cut his fat, loose cheeks in two. His other
ear remained free. Cropped close to his head in the shape
of a little paper screw-bag, this ear was the watchful re-
ceiver into which all the sounds of life fell, like pebbles disturbing its rest.

He had also encased his hind-legs in a pair of patent-
leather riding-boots, with white tops; but his fore-paws he
considered of such use that nothing would have induced him
to put them into gloves. Tylô had too natural a character
to change his little ways all in a day; and, in spite of his

new-blown honours, he allowed himself to do undignified things. He was at the present moment lying on the steps of the hall, scratching the ground and sniffing at the wall, when suddenly he gave a start and began to whine and whimper! His lower lip shook nervously as though he were going to cry.

"What's the matter with the idiot now?" asked the Cat, who was watching him out of the corner of her eye.

But she at once understood. A very sweet song came from the distance; and Tylô could not endure music. The song drew nearer, a girl's fresh voice filled the shadows of the lofty arches and Water appeared. Tall, slender and white as a pearl, she seemed to glide rather than to walk. Her movements were so soft and graceful that they were suspected rather than seen. A beautiful silvery dress waved and floated around her; and her hair decked with corals flowed below her knees.

When Fire caught sight of her, like the rude and spiteful fellow that he was, he sneered:

"She's not brought her umbrella!"

But Water, who was really quite witty and who knew that she was the stronger of the two, chaffed him pleasantly and said, with a glance at his glowing nose:

"I beg your pardon? . . . I thought you might be speaking of a great red nose I saw the other day! . . ."

The others began to laugh and poke fun at Fire, whose face was always like a red-hot coal. Fire angrily jumped to the ceiling, keeping his revenge for later. Meanwhile, the Cat went up to Water, very cautiously, and paid her ever so many compliments on her dress. I need hardly tell you that she did not mean a word of it; but she wished to be friendly with everybody, for she wanted their votes, to carry out her plan; and she was anxious at not seeing Bread, because she did not want to speak before the meeting was complete:

"What can he be doing?" she mewed, time after time.

"He was making an endless fuss about choosing his dress," said the Dog. "At last, he decided in favour of a Turkish robe, with a scimitar and a turban."

The words were not out of his mouth, when a shapeless and ridiculous bulk, clad in all the colours of the rainbow, came and blocked the narrow door of the hall. It was the enormous stomach of Bread, who filled the whole opening. He kept on knocking himself, without knowing why; for he was not very clever and, besides, he was not yet used to moving about in human beings' houses. At

last, it occurred to him to stoop; and, by squeezing through
sideways, he managed to make his way into the hall.

It was certainly not a triumphal entry, but he was pleased
with it all the same:

"Here I am!" he said. "Here I am! I have put on Blue-
beard's finest dress. . . . What do you think of this?"

The Dog began to frisk around him: he thought Bread
magnificent! That yellow velvet costume, covered all
over with silver crescents, reminded Tylô of the delicious
horse-shoe rolls which he loved; and the huge, gaudy turban
on Bread's head was really very like a fairy bun!

"How nice he looks!" he cried. "How nice he looks!"

Bread was shyly followed by Milk. Her simple mind
had made her prefer her cream dress to all the finery which
the Fairy suggested to her. She was really a model of
humility.

Bread was beginning to talk about the dresses of Tyltyl,
Light and Mytyl, when the Cat cut him short in a masterful
voice:

"We shall see them in good time," she said. "Stop chattering, listen to me, time presses: our future is at stake. . ."

They all looked at her with a bewildered air. They understood that it was a solemn moment, but the human lan-

guage was still full of mystery to them. Sugar wriggled
his long fingers as a sign of distress; Bread patted his huge
stomach; Water lay on the floor and seemed to suffer from
the most profound despair; and Milk only had eyes for
Bread, who had been her friend for ages and ages.

The Cat, becoming impatient, continued her speech:

"The Fairy has just said it, the end of this journey will,
at the same time, mark the end of our lives. It is our
business, therefore, to spin the journey out as long as possible and by every means in our power. . . ."

Bread, who was afraid of being eaten as soon as he was
no longer a man, hastened to express approval; but the Dog,
who was standing a little way off, pretending not to hear,
began to growl deep down in his soul. He well knew what
the Cat was driving at; and, when Tylette ended her speech
with the words, "We must at all costs prolong the journey
and prevent Blue Bird from being found, even if it means
endangering the lives of the Children," the good Dog, obey-
ing only the promptings of his heart, leapt at the Cat to
bite her. Sugar, Bread and Fire flung themselves between
them:

"Order! Order!" said Bread pompously. "I'm in the
chair at this meeting."

"Who made you chairman?" stormed Fire.

"Who asked you to interfere?" asked Water, whirling her wet hair over Fire.

"Excuse me," said Sugar, shaking all over, in conciliatory tones. "Excuse me. . . . This is a serious moment. . . . Let us talk things over in a friendly way."

"I quite agree with Sugar and the Cat," said Bread, as though that ended the matter.

"This is ridiculous!" said the Dog, barking and showing his teeth. "There is Man and that's all! . . . We have to obey him and do as he tells us! . . . I recognise no one but him! . . . Hurrah for Man! . . . Man for ever! . . . In life or death, all for Man! . . . Man is everything! . . ."

But the Cat's shrill voice rose above all the others. She was full of grudges against Man and she wanted to make use of the short spell of humanity which she now enjoyed to avenge her whole race:

"All of us here present." she cried, "Animals, Things and Elements, possess a soul which Man does not yet know. That is why we retain a remnant of independence; but, if he finds the Blue Bird, he will know all, he will see all and we shall be completely at his mercy. . . . Remember the time when we wandered at liberty upon the face of the earth! . . ." But, suddenly her face changed, her voice sank to a whisper and she hissed, "Look out! I hear the

Fairy and Light coming. I need hardly tell you that Light has taken sides with Man and means to stand by him; she is our worst enemy. . . . Be careful!"

But our friends had had no practice in trickery and, feeling themselves in the wrong, took up such ridiculous and uncomfortable attitudes that the Fairy, the moment she appeared upon the threshold, exclaimed:

"What are you doing in that corner? . . . You look like a pack of conspirators!"

Quite scared and thinking that the Fairy had already guessed their wicked intentions, they fell upon their knees before her. Luckily for them, the Fairy hardly gave a thought to what was passing through their little minds. She had come to explain the first part of the journey to the Children and to tell each of the others what to do. Tyltyl and Mytyl stood hand in hand in front of her, looking a little frightened and a little awkward in their fine clothes. They stared at each other in childish admiration.

The little girl was wearing a yellow silk frock embroidered with pink posies and covered with gold spangles. On her head was a lovely orange velvet cap; and a starched muslin tucker covered her little arms. Tyltyl was dressed in a red jacket and blue knickerbockers, both of velvet; and of course he wore the wonderful little hat on his head.

The Fairy said to them:

"It is just possible that the Blue Bird is hiding at your grandparents' in the Land of Memory; so you will go there first."

"But how shall we see them, if they are dead?" asked Tyltyl.

Then the good Fairy explained that they would not be really dead until their grandchildren ceased to think of them:

"Men do not know this secret," she added. "But, thanks to the diamond, you, Tyltyl, will see that the dead whom we remember live as happily as though they were not dead."

"Are you coming with us?" asked the boy, turning to Light, who stood in the doorway and lit up all the hall.

"No," said the Fairy. "Light must not look at the past. Her energies must be devoted to the future!"

The two Children were starting on their way, when they discovered that they were very hungry. The Fairy at once ordered Bread to give them something to eat; and that big, fat fellow, delighted with the importance of his duty, undid the top of his robe, drew his scimitar and cut two slices out of his stomach. The Children screamed with laughter. Tylô dropped his gloomy thoughts for a moment and begged for a bit of bread; and everybody struck up the farewell chorus. Sugar, who was very full of himself, also wanted to impress the company and, breaking off two of his fingers, handed them to the astonished Children.

As they were all moving towards the door, the Fairy Bérylune stopped them:

"Not to-day," she said. "The children must go alone. It would be indiscreet to accompany them; they are going to spend the evening with their late family. Come, be off! Good-bye, dear children, and mind that you are back in good time: it is extremely important!"

The two Children took each other by the hand and, carry-ing the big cage, passed out of the hall; and their com-panions, at a sign from the Fairy, filed in front of her to return to the palace. Our friend Tylô was the only one who did not answer to his name. The moment he heard the Fairy say that the Children were to go alone, he had made up his mind to go and look after them, whatever hap-pened; and, while the others were saying good-bye, he hid behind the door. But the poor fellow had reckoned without the all-seeing eyes of the Fairy Bérylune.

"Tylô!" she cried. "Tylô! Here!"

And the poor Dog, who had so long been used to obey, dared not resist the command and came, with his tail between his legs, to take his place among the others. He howled with despair when he saw his little master and mistress swallowed up in the great gold staircase.

The Land of Memory

CHAPTER III

THE Fairy Bérylune had told the Children that the Land of Memory was not far off; but to reach it you had to go through a forest that was so dense and so old that your eyes could not see the tops of the trees. It was always shrouded in a heavy mist; and the Children would certainly have lost their way, if the Fairy had not said to them beforehand:

"It is straight ahead; and there is only one road."

The ground was carpeted with flowers which were all alike: they were snow-white pansies and very pretty; but, as they never saw the sun, they had no scent.

Those little flowers comforted the Children, who felt extremely lonely. A great mysterious silence surrounded them; and they trembled a little with a very pleasant sense of fear which they had never felt before.

"Let's take Granny a bunch of flowers," said Mytyl.

"That's a good idea! She will be pleased!" cried Tyltyl.

And, as they walked along, the Children gathered a beautiful white nosegay. The dear little things did not know that every pansy (which means "a thought") that they picked brought them nearer to their grandparents; and they soon saw before them a large oak with a notice-board nailed to it.

"Here we are!" cried the boy in triumph, as, climbing up on a root, he read:

"The Land of Memory."

They had arrived; but they turned to every side without seeing a thing:

"I can see nothing at all!" whimpered Mytyl. "I'm cold! . . . I'm tired! . . . I don't want to travel any more!"

Tyltyl, who was wholly wrapped up in his errand, lost his temper:

"Come, don't keep on crying just like Water! . . . You ought to be ashamed of yourself!" he said. "There! Look! Look! The fog is lifting!"

And, sure enough, the mist parted before their eyes, like veils torn by an invisible hand; the big trees faded away, everything vanished and, instead, there appeared a pretty little peasant's cottage, covered with creepers and standing in a little garden filled with flowers and with trees all over fruit.

The Children at once knew the dear cow in the orchard, the watch-dog at the door, the blackbird in his wicker cage; and everything was steeped in a pale light and a warm and balmy air.

Tyltyl and Mytyl stood amazed. So that was the Land of Memory! What lovely weather it was! And how nice it felt to be there! They at once made up their minds to come back often, now that they knew the way. But how great was their happiness when the last veil disappeared and they saw, at a few steps from them, Grandad and Granny sitting on a bench, sound asleep. They clapped their hands and called out gleefully:

"It's Grandad! It's Granny! . . . There they are! There they are!"

But they were a little scared by this great piece of magic and dared not move from behind the tree; and they stood looking at the dear old couple, who woke up gently and slowly under their eyes. Then they heard Granny Tyl's quavering voice say:

"I have a notion that our grandchildren who are still alive are coming to see us to-day."

And Gaffer Tyl answered:

"They are certainly thinking of us, for I feel anyhow and I have pins and needles in my legs."

"I think they must be quite near," said Granny, "for I see tears of joy dancing before my eyes and . . ."

Granny had not time to finish her sentence. The Children were in her arms! . . . What joy! What wild kisses and huggings! What a wonderful surprise! The happiness was too great for words. They laughed and tried to speak and kept on looking at one another with delighted eyes: it was so glorious and so unexpected to meet again like this. When the first excitement was over, they all began to talk at once:

"How tall and strong you've grown, Tyltyl!" said Granny.

And Grandad cried:

"And Mytyl! Just look at her! What pretty hair, what pretty eyes!"

And the Children danced and clapped their hands and flung themselves by turns into the arms of one or the other.

At last, they quieted down a little; and, with Mytyl nestling against Grandad's chest and Tyltyl comfortably perched on Granny's knees, they began to talk of family affairs:

"How are Daddy and Mummy Tyl?" asked Granny.

"Quite well, Granny," said Tyltyl. "They were asleep when we went out."

Granny gave them fresh kisses and said:

"My word, how pretty they are and how nice and clean! . . . Why don't you come to see us oftener? It is months and months now that you have forgotten us and that we have seen nobody. . . ."

"We couldn't, Granny," said Tyltyl, "and to-day it's only because of the Fairy . . ."

"We are always here," said Granny Tyl, "waiting for a visit from those who are alive. The last time you were here was on All-hallows. . . ."

"All-hallows? We didn't go out that day, for we both had colds!"

"But you thought of us! And, every time you think of us, we wake up and see you again."

Tyltyl remembered that the Fairy had told him this. He had not thought it possible then; but now, with his head on the heart of the dear Granny whom he had missed so much, he began to understand things and he felt that his grandparents had not left him altogether. He asked:

"So you are not really dead? . . ."

The old couple burst out laughing. When they exchanged their life on earth for another and a much nicer and more beautiful life, they had forgotten the word "dead."

"What does that word 'dead' mean?" asked Gaffer Tyl.

"Why, it means that one's no longer alive!" said Tyltyl.

Grandad and Granny only shrugged their shoulders:

"How stupid the Living are, when they speak of the Others!" was all they said.

And they went over their memories again, rejoicing in being able to chat.

All old people love discussing old times. The future is finished, as far as they are concerned; and so they delight in the present and the past. But we are growing impatient, like Tyltyl; and, instead of listening to them, we will follow our little friend's movements.

He had jumped off Granny's knees and was poking about in every corner, delighted at finding all sorts of things which he knew and remembered:

"Nothing is changed, everything is in its old place!" he cried. And, as he had not been to the old people's home for so long, everything struck him as much nicer; and he added, in the voice of one who knows, "Only everything is prettier! . . . Hullo, there's the clock with the big hand which I broke the point off and the hole which I made in the door, the day I found Grandad's gimlet. . . ."

"Yes, you've done some damage in your time!" said

Grandad. "And there's the plum-tree which you were so fond of climbing, when I wasn't looking. . . ."

Meantime, Tyltyl was not forgetting his errand:

"You haven't the Blue Bird here by chance, I suppose?"

At the same moment, Mytyl, lifting her head, saw a cage:

"Hullo, there's the old blackbird! . . . Does he still sing?"

As she spoke, the blackbird woke up and began to sing at the top of his voice.

"You see," said Granny, "as soon as one thinks of him . . ."

Tyltyl was simply amazed at what he saw:

"But he's blue!" he shouted. "Why, that's the bird, the Blue Bird! . . . He's blue, blue, blue as a blue glass marble! . . . Will you give him to me?"

The grandparents gladly consented; and, full of triumph, Tyltyl went and fetched the cage which he had left by the tree. He took hold of the precious bird with the greatest of care; and it began to hop about in its new home.

"How pleased the Fairy will be!" said the boy, rejoicing at his conquest. "And Light too!"

"Come along," said the grandparents. "Come and look at the cow and the bees."

As the old couple were beginning to toddle across the

garden, the children suddenly asked if their little dead brothers and sisters were there too. At the same moment, seven little children, who, up to then, had been sleeping in the house, came tearing like mad into the garden. Tyltyl and Mytyl ran up to them. They all hustled and hugged one another and danced and whirled about and uttered screams of joy.

"Here they are, here they are!" said Granny. "As soon as you speak of them, they are there, the imps!"

Tyltyl caught a little one by the hair:

"Hullo, Pierrot! So we're going to fight again, as in the old days! . . . And Robert! . . . I say, Jean, what's become of your top? . . . Madeleine and Pierrette and Pauline! . . . And here's Riquette! . . ."

Mytyl laughed:

"Riquette's still crawling on all fours!"

Tyltyl noticed a little dog yapping around them:

"There's Kiki, whose tail I cut off with Pauline's scissors. . . . He hasn't changed either. . . ."

"No," said Gaffer Tyl, in a voice of great importance, "nothing changes here!"

But, suddenly, amid the general rejoicings, the old people stopped spell-bound: they had heard the small voice of the clock indoors strike eight!

"How's this?" they asked. "It never strikes nowadays. . . ."

"That's because we no longer think of the time," said Granny. "Was any one thinking of the time?"

"Yes, I was," said Tyltyl. "So it's eight o'clock? . . . Then I'm off, for I promised Light to be back before nine. . . ."

He was going for the cage, but the others were too happy to let him run away so soon: it would be horrid to say good-bye like that! Granny had a good idea: she knew what a little glutton Tyltyl was. It was just supper-time and, as luck would have it, there was some capital cabbage-soup and a beautiful plum-tart.

"Well," said our hero, "as I've got the Blue Bird! . . . And cabbage-soup is a thing you don't have every day! . . ."

They all hurried and carried the table outside and laid it with a nice white table-cloth and put a plate for each; and, lastly, Granny brought out the steaming soup-tureen in state. The lamp was lit and the grandparents and grandchildren sat down to supper, jostling and elbowing one another and laughing and shouting with pleasure. Then, for a time, nothing was heard but the sound of the wooden spoons noisily clattering against the soup-plates.

"How good it is! Oh, how good it is!" shouted Tyltyl, who was eating greedily. "I want some more! More! More! More!"

"Come, come, a little more quiet," said Grandad. "You're just as ill-behaved as ever; and you'll break your plate. . . ."

Tyltyl took no notice of the remark, stood up on his stool, caught hold of the tureen and dragged it towards him and upset it; and the hot soup trickled all over the table and down upon everybody's lap. The children yelled and screamed with pain. Granny was quite scared; and Grandad was furious. He dealt our friend Tyltyl a tremendous box on the ear.

Tyltyl was staggered for a moment; and then he put his hand to his cheek with a look of rapture and exclaimed:

"Grandad, how good, how jolly! It was just like the slaps you used to give me when you were alive! . . I must give you a kiss for it! . . ."

Everybody laughed.

"There's more where that came from, if you like them!" said Grandad, grumpily.

But he was touched, all the same, and turned to wipe a tear from his eyes.

"Goodness!" cried Tyltyl, starting up. "There's half-past eight striking! . . . Mytyl, we've only just got time! . . ."

Granny in vain implored them to stay a few minutes longer.

"No, we can't possibly," said Tyltyl firmly; "I promised Light!"

And he hurried to take up the precious cage.

"Good-bye, Grandad. . . . Good-bye, Granny. . . . Good-bye, brothers and sisters, Pierrot, Robert, Pauline, Madeleine, Riquette and you, too, Kiki. . . . We can't stay. . . . Don't cry, Granny; we will come back often!"

Poor old Grandad was very much upset and complained lustily:

"Gracious me, how tiresome the Living are, with all their fuss and excitement!"

Tyltyl tried to console him and again promised to come back very often.

"Come back every day!" said Granny. "It is our only pleasure; and it's such a treat for us when your thoughts pay us a visit!"

"Good-bye! Good-bye!" cried the brothers and sisters in chorus. "Come back very soon! Bring us some barley sugar!"

There were more kisses; all waved their handkerchiefs;

all shouted a last good-bye. But the figures began to fade
away; the little voices could no longer be heard; the two
Children were once more wrapped in mist; and the old forest
covered them with its great dark mantle.

"I'm so frightened!" whimpered Mytyl. "Give me your
hand, little brother! I'm so frightened!"

Tyltyl was shaking too, but it was his duty to try and
comfort and console his sister:

"Hush!" he said. "Remember that we are bringing back
the Blue Bird!"

As he spoke, a thin ray of light pierced the gloom; and
the little boy hurried towards it. He was holding his cage
tight in his arms; and the first thing he did was to look
at his bird. . . . Alas and alack, what a disappointment
awaited him! The beautiful Blue Bird of the Land of
Memory had turned quite black! Stare at it as hard as
Tyltyl might, the bird was black! Oh, how well he knew
the old blackbird that used to sing in its wicker prison, in
the old days, at the door of the house! What had happened? How painful it was! And how cruel life seemed
to him just then!

He had started on his journey with such zest and delight
that he had not thought for a moment of the difficulties
and dangers. Full of confidence, pluck and kindness, he

had marched off, certain of finding the beautiful Blue Bird which would bring happiness to the Fairy's little girl. And now all his hopes were shattered! For the first time, our poor friend perceived the mortifications, the vexations, the obstacles that awaited him! Alas, was he attempting an impossible thing? Was the Fairy making fun of him? Would he ever find the Blue Bird? All his courage seemed to be leaving him. . . .

To add to his misfortunes, he could not find the straight road by which he had come. There was not a single white pansy on the ground; and he began to cry.

Luckily, our little friends were not to remain in trouble long. The Fairy had promised that Light would watch over them. The first trial was over; and, just as outside the old people's house a little while ago, the mist now suddenly lifted. But, instead of disclosing a peaceful picture, a gentle, homely scene, it revealed a marvellous temple, with a blinding glare streaming from it.

On the threshold stood Light, fair and beautiful in her diamond-coloured dress. She smiled when Tyltyl told her of his first failure. She knew what the little ones were seeking; she knew everything. For Light surrounds all mortals with her love, though none of them is fond enough of her ever to receive her thoroughly and thus to learn all

the secrets of Truth. Now, for the first time, thanks to
the diamond which the Fairy had given to the boy, she was
going to try and conquer a human soul:

"Do not be sad," she said to the Children. "Are you not
pleased to have seen your grandparents? Is that not
enough happiness for one day? Are you not glad to have
restored the old blackbird to life? Listen to him singing!"

For the old blackbird was singing with might and main;
and his little yellow eyes sparkled with pleasure as he
hopped about his big cage.

"As you look for the Blue Bird, dear Children, accustom
yourselves to love the grey birds which you find on your
way."

She nodded her fair head gravely; and it was quite clear
that she knew where the Blue Bird was. But life is often
full of beautiful mysteries, which we must respect, lest we
should destroy them; and, if Light had told the Children
where the Blue Bird was, well, they would never have
found him! I will tell you why at the end of this story.

And now let us leave our little friends to sleep on beautiful white clouds under Light's watchful care.

The Palace of Night

CHAPTER IV

THE PALACE OF NIGHT

SOME time after, the Children and their friends met at the first dawn to go to the Palace of Night, where they hoped to find the Blue Bird. Several of the party failed to answer to their names when the roll was called. Milk, for whom any sort of excitement was bad, was keeping her room. Water sent an excuse: she was accustomed always to travel in a bed of moss, was already half-dead with fatigue and was afraid of falling ill. As for Light, she had been on bad terms with Night since the world began; and Fire, as a relation, shared her dislike. Light kissed the Children and told Tylô the way, for it was his business to lead the expedition; and the little band set out upon its road.

You can imagine dear Tylô trotting ahead, on his hind-legs, like a little man, with his nose in the air, his tongue dangling down his chin, his front paws folded across his chest. He fidgets, sniffs about, runs up and down, covering twice the ground without minding how tired it makes him.

65

He is so full of his own importance that he disdains the temptations on his path: he neglects the rubbish-heaps, pays no attention to anything he sees and cuts all his old friends.

Poor Tylô! He was so delighted to become a man; and yet he was no happier than before! Of course, life was the same to him, because his nature had remained unchanged. What was the use of his being a man, if he continued to feel and think like a dog? In fact, his troubles were increased a hundred-fold by the sense of responsibility that now weighed upon him.

"Ah!" he said, with a sigh, for he was joining blindly in his little gods' search, without for a moment reflecting that the end of the journey would mean the end of his life. "Ah," he said, "if I got hold of that rascal of a Blue Bird, trust me, I wouldn't touch him even with the tip of my tongue, not if he were as plump and sweet as a quail!"

Bread followed solemnly, carrying the cage; the two Children came next; and Sugar brought up the rear.

But where was the Cat? To discover the reason of her absence, we must go a little way back and read her thoughts. At the time when Tylette called a meeting of the Animals and Things in the Fairy's hall, she was contemplating a great plot which would aim at prolonging the journey; but she had reckoned without the stupidity of her hearers:

"The idiots," she thought, "have very nearly spoilt the whole thing by foolishly throwing themselves at the Fairy's feet, as though they were guilty of a crime. It is better to rely upon one's self alone. In my cat-life, all our training is founded on suspicion; I can see that it is just the same in the life of men. Those who confide in others are only betrayed; it is better to keep silent and to be treacherous one's self."

As you see, my dear little readers, the Cat was in the same position as the Dog: she had not changed her soul and was simply continuing her former existence; but, of course, she was very wicked, whereas our dear Tylô was, if anything, too good. Tylette, therefore, resolved to act on her own account and went, before daybreak, to call on Night, who was an old friend of hers.

The road to the Palace of Night was rather long and rather dangerous. It had precipices on either side of it; you had to climb up and climb down and then climb up again among high rocks that always seemed waiting to crush the passers-by. At last, you came to the edge of a dark circus; and there you had to go down thousands of steps to reach the black-marble underground palace in which Night lived.

The Cat, who had often been there before, raced along

the road, light as a feather. Her cloak, borne on the wind, streamed like a banner behind her; the plume in her hat fluttered gracefully; and her little grey kid boots hardly touched the ground. She soon reached her destination and, in a few bounds, came to the great hall where Night was.

It was really a wonderful sight. Night, stately and grand as a Queen, reclined upon her throne; she slept; and not a glimmer, not a star twinkled around her. But we know that the night has no secrets for cats and that their eyes have the power of piercing the darkness. So Tylette saw Night as though it were broad daylight.

Before waking her, she cast a loving glance at that motherly and familiar face. It was white and silvery as the moon; and its unbending features inspired both fear and admiration. Night's figure, which was half visible through her long black veils, was as beautiful as that of a Greek statue. She had no arms; but a pair of enormous wings, now furled in sleep, came from her shoulders to her feet and gave her a look of majesty beyond compare. Still, in spite of her affection for her best of friends, Tylette did not waste too much time in gazing at her: it was a critical moment; and time was short. Tired and jaded and overcome with anguish, she sank upon the steps of the throne and mewed, plaintively:

"It is I, Mother Night! . . . I am worn out!"

Night is of an anxious nature and easily alarmed. Her
beauty, built up of peace and repose, possesses the secret of
Silence, which life is constantly disturbing: a star shooting
through the sky, a leaf falling to the ground, the hoot of an
owl, a mere nothing is enough to tear the black velvet pall
which she spreads over the earth each evening. The Cat,
therefore, had not finished speaking, when Night sat up,
all quivering. Her immense wings beat around her; and
she questioned Tylette in a trembling voice. As soon as
she had learnt the danger that threatened her, she began
to lament her fate. What! A man's son coming to her palace! And, perhaps, with the help of the magic diamond,
discovering her secrets! What should she do? What
would become of her? How could she defend herself?
And, forgetting that she was sinning against Silence, her
own particular god, Night began to utter piercing screams.
It was true that falling into such a commotion was hardly
likely to help her find a cure for her troubles. Luckily for
her, Tylette, who was accustomed to the annoyances and
worries of human life, was better armed. She had worked
out her plan when going ahead of the children; and she was
hoping to persuade Night to adopt it. She explained this
plan to her in a few words:

"I see only one thing for it, Mother Night: as they are children, we must give them such a fright that they will not dare to insist on opening the great door at the back of the hall, behind which the Birds of the Moon live and generally the Blue Bird too. The secrets of the other caverns will be sure to scare them. The hope of our safety lies in the terror which you will make them feel."

There was clearly no other course to take. But Night had not time to reply, for she heard a sound. Then her beautiful features contracted; her wings spread out angrily; and everything in her attitude told Tylette that Night approved of her plan.

"Here they are!" cried the Cat.

The little band came marching down the steps of Night's gloomy staircase. Tylô pranced bravely in front, whereas Tyltyl looked around him with an anxious glance. He certainly found nothing to comfort him. It was all very magnificent, but very terrifying. Picture a huge and wonderful black marble hall, of a stern and tomb-like splendour. There is no ceiling visible; and the ebony pillars that surround the amphitheatre shoot up to the sky. It is only when you lift your eyes up there that you catch the faint light falling from the stars. Everywhere, the thickest darkness reigns. Two restless flames—no more—flicker on either side of Night's throne, before a monumental door of brass. Bronze doors show through the pillars to the right and left.

The Cat rushed up to the Children:

"This way, little master, this way! . . . I have told Night; and she is delighted to see you."

Tylette's soft voice and smile made Tyltyl feel himself again; and he walked up to the throne with a bold and confident step, saying:

"Good-day, Mrs. Night!"

Night was offended by the word, "Good-day," which reminded her of her eternal enemy Light, and answered drily:

"Good-day? . . . I am not used to that! . . . You might say, Good-night, or, at least, Good-evening!"

Our hero was not prepared to quarrel. He felt very small in the presence of that stately lady. He quickly begged her pardon, as nicely as he could; and very gently asked her leave to look for the Blue Bird in her palace.

"I have never seen him, he is not here!" exclaimed Night, flapping her great wings to frighten the boy.

But, when he insisted and gave no sign of fear, she herself began to dread the diamond. which, by lighting up her darkness, would completely destroy her power; and she thought it better to pretend to yield to an impulse of generosity and at once to point to the big key that lay on the steps of the throne.

Without a moment's hesitation, Tyltyl seized hold of it and ran to the first door of the hall.

Everybody shook with fright. Bread's teeth chattered in his head; Sugar, who was standing some way off, moaned with mortal anguish; Mytyl howled:

"Where is Sugar? . . . I want to go home!"

Meanwhile, Tyltyl, pale and resolute, was trying to open the door, while Night's grave voice, rising above the din, proclaimed the first danger.

"It's the Ghosts!"

"Oh, dear!" thought Tyltyl. "I have never seen a ghost: it must be awful!"

The faithful Tylô, by his side, was panting with all his might, for dogs hate anything uncanny.

At last, the key grated in the lock. Silence reigned as dense and heavy as the darkness. No one dared draw a breath. Then the door opened; and, in a moment, the gloom was filled with white figures running in every direction. Some lengthened out right up to the sky; others twined themselves round the pillars; others wriggled ever so fast along the ground. They were something like men, but it was impossible to distinguish their features; the eye could not catch them. The moment you looked at them, they turned into a white mist. Tyltyl did his best to chase them; for Mrs. Night kept to the plan contrived by the Cat and pretended to be frightened. She had been the Ghosts' friend for hundreds and hundreds of years and had only to say a word to drive them in again; but she was careful to do nothing of the sort and, flapping her wings like mad, she called upon all her gods and screamed:

"Drive them away! Drive them away! Help! Help!"

But the poor Ghosts, who hardly ever come out now that Man no longer believes in them, were much too happy at taking a breath of air; and, had it not been that they were afraid of Tylô, who tried to bite their legs, they would never have been got indoors.

"Oof!" gasped the Dog, when the door was shut at last. "I have strong teeth, goodness knows; but chaps like those I never saw before! When you bite them, you'd think their legs were made of cotton!"

By this time, Tyltyl was making for the second door and asking:

"What's behind this one?"

Night made a gesture as though to put him off. Did the obstinate little fellow really want to see everything?

"Must I be careful when I open it?" asked Tyltyl.

"No," said Night, "it is not worth while. It's the Sick-nesses. They are very quiet, the poor little things! Man, for some time, has been waging such war upon them! . . . Open and see for yourself. . . ."

Tyltyl threw the door wide open and stood speechless with astonishment: there was nothing to be seen. . . .

He was just about to close the door again, when he was hustled aside by a little body in a dressing-gown and a cotton night-cap, who began to frisk about the hall, wagging her head and stopping every minute to cough, sneeze and blow her nose . . . and to pull on her slippers, which were too big for her and kept dropping off her feet. Sugar, Bread and Tyltyl were no longer frightened and began to laugh like anything. But they had no sooner come near the little person in the cotton night-cap than they themselves began to cough and sneeze.

"It's the least important of the Sicknesses," said Night. "It's Cold-in-the-Head."

"Oh, dear, oh, dear!" thought Sugar. "If my nose keeps on running like this, I'm done for: I shall melt!"

Poor Sugar! He did not know where to hide himself. He had become very much attached to life since the journey began, for he had fallen over head and ears in love with Water! And yet this love caused him the greatest worry.

Miss Water was a tremendous flirt, expected a lot of attention and was not particular whom she mixed with; but mixing too much with Water was an expensive luxury, as poor Sugar found to his cost; for, at every kiss he gave her, he left a bit of himself behind, until he began to tremble for his life.

When he suddenly found himself attacked by Cold-in-the-Head, he would have had to fly from the palace, but for the timely aid of our dear Tylô, who ran after the little minx and drove her back to her cavern, amidst the laughter of Tyltyl and Mytyl, who thought gleefully that, so far, the trial had not been very terrible.

The boy, therefore, ran to the next door with still greater courage.

"Take care!" cried Night, in a dreadful voice. "It's the Wars! They are more powerful than ever! I daren't think what would happen, if one of them broke loose! Stand ready, all of you, to push back the door!"

Night had not finished uttering her warnings, when the plucky little fellow repented his rashness. He tried in vain to shut the door which he had opened: an invincible force was pushing it from the other side, streams of blood flowed through the cracks; flames shot forth; shouts, oaths and groans mingled with the roar of cannon and the rattle of musketry. Everybody in the Palace of Night was running about in wild confusion. Bread and Sugar tried to take to flight, but could not find the way out; and they now came back to Tyltyl and put their shoulders to the door with despairing force.

The Cat pretended to be anxious, while secretly rejoicing:

"This may be the end of it," she said, curling her whiskers. "They won't dare to go on after this."

Dear Tylô made superhuman efforts to help his little master, while Mytyl stood crying in a corner.

At last, our hero gave a shout of triumph:

"Hurrah' They're giving way! Victory! Victory! The door is shut!"

At the same time, he dropped on the steps, utterly exhausted, dabbing his forehead with his poor little hands which shook with terror.

"Well?" asked Night, harshly. "Have you had enough? Did you see them?"

"Yes, yes!" replied the little fellow, sobbing. "They are hideous and awful. . . . I don't think they have the Blue Bird." . . .

"You may be sure they haven't," answered Night, angrily. "If they had, they would eat him at once. . . . You see there is nothing to be done. . . ."

Tyltyl drew himself up proudly:

"I must see everything," he declared. "Light said so. . . ."

"It's an easy thing to say," retorted Night, "when one's afraid and stays at home!"

"Let us go to the next door," said Tyltyl, resolutely. "What's in here?"

"This is where I keep the Shades and the Terrors!"

Tyltyl reflected for a minute:

"As far as Shades go," he thought, "Mrs. Night is poking fun at me. It's more than an hour since I've seen anything but shade in this house of hers; and I shall be very glad to see daylight again. As for the Terrors, if they are anything like the Ghosts, we shall have another good joke."

Our friend went to the door and opened it, before his companions had time to protest. For that matter, they were all sitting on the floor, exhausted with the last fright; and they looked at one another in astonishment, glad to find themselves alive after such a scare. Meanwhile, Tyltyl threw back the door and nothing came out:

"There's no one there!" he said.

"Yes, there is! Yes, there is! Look out!" said Night, who was still shamming fright.

She was simply furious. She had hoped to make a great

impression with her Terrors; and, lo and behold, the
wretches, who had so long been snubbed by Man, were
afraid of him! She encouraged them with kind words
and succeeded in coaxing out a few tall figures covered with
grey veils. They began to run all around the hall until,
hearing the Children laugh, they were seized with fear and
rushed indoors again. The attempt had failed, as far as
Night was concerned, and the dread hour was about to
strike. Already, Tyltyl was moving towards the big door
at the end of the hall. A few last words took place between
them:

"Do not open that one!" said Night, in awe-struck tones.

"Why not?"

"Because it's not allowed!"

"Then it's here that the Blue Bird is hidden!"

"Go no farther, do not tempt fate, do not open that door!"

"But why?" again asked Tyltyl, obstinately.

Thereupon, Night, irritated by his persistency, flew into
a rage, hurled the most terrible threats at him, and ended by
saying:

"Not one of those who have opened it, were it but by a
hair's breadth, has ever returned alive to the light of day!
It means certain death; and all the horrors, all the terrors,
all the fears of which men speak on earth are as nothing com-

pared with those which await you if you insist on touching that door!"

"Don't do it, master dear!" said Bread, with chattering teeth. "Don't do it! Take pity on us! I implore you on my knees!"

"You are sacrificing the lives of all of us," mewed the Cat.

"I won't! I sha'n't!" sobbed Mytyl.

"Pity! Pity!" whined Sugar, wringing his fingers.

All of them were weeping and crying, all of them crowded round Tyltyl. Dear Tylô alone, who respected his little master's wishes, dared not speak a word, though he fully believed that his last hour had come. Two big tears rolled down his cheeks; and he licked Tyltyl's hands in despair. It was really a most touching scene; and for a moment, our hero hesitated. His heart beat wildly, his throat was parched with anguish, he tried to speak and could not get out a sound: besides, he did not wish to show weakness in the presence of his hapless companions!

"If I have not the strength to fulfil my task," he said to himself, "who will fulfil it? If my friends behold my distress, it is all up with me: they will not let me go through with my mission and I shall never find the Blue Bird!"

At this thought, the boy's heart leapt within his breast and all his generous nature rose in rebellion. It would never do to be, perhaps, within arm's length of happiness and not to try for it, at the risk of dying in the attempt, to try for it and hand it over at last to all mankind!

That settled it! Tyltyl resolved to sacrifice himself. Like a true hero, he brandished the heavy golden key and cried:

"I must open the door!"

He ran up to the great door, with Tylô panting by his side. The poor Dog was half-dead with fright, but his pride and his devotion to Tyltyl obliged him to smother his fears:

"I shall stay," he said to his master, "I'm not afraid! I shall stay with my little god!"

In the meantime, all the others had fled. Bread was crumbling to bits behind a pillar; Sugar was melting in a corner with Mytyl in his arms; Night and the Cat, both shaking with fury, kept to the far end of the hall.

Then Tyltyl gave Tylô a last kiss, pressed him to his heart and, with never a tremble, put the key in the lock. Yells of terror came from all the corners of the hall, where the runaways had taken shelter, while the two leaves of the great door opened by magic in front of our little friend, who was struck dumb with admiration and delight. What an exquisite surprise! A wonderful garden lay before him, a dream-garden filled with flowers that shone like stars, waterfalls that came rushing from the sky and trees which the moon had clothed in silver. And then there was something whirling like a blue cloud among the clusters of roses. Tyltyl rubbed his eyes, could not believe his senses. He waited, looked again and then dashed into the garden, shouting like mad:

"Come quickly! . . . Come quickly! . . . They are here! . . . We have them at last! . . . Millions of blue birds! . . . Thousands of millions! . . . Come, Mytyl! . . . Come, Tylô! . . . Come, all! . . . Help me! . . . You can catch them by handfuls! . . ."

Reassured at last, his friends came running up and all darted in among the birds, seeing who could catch the most:

"I've caught seven already!" cried Mytyl. "I can't hold them!"

"Nor can I!" said Tyltyl. "I have too many of them! . . . They're escaping from my arms! . . . Tylô has some too! . . . Let us go out, let us go! . . . Light is waiting for us! . . . How pleased she will be! . . . This way, this way! . . ."

And they all danced and scampered away in their glee, singing songs of triumph as they went.

Night and the Cat, who had not shared in the general rejoicing, crept back anxiously to the great door; and Night whimpered:

"Haven't they got him? . . ."

"No," said the Cat, who saw the real Blue Bird perched high up on a moonbeam. . . . "They could not reach him, he kept too high. . . ."

Our friends in all haste ran up the numberless stairs between them and the daylight. Each of them hugged the birds which he had captured, never dreaming that every step which brought them nearer to the light was fatal to the poor things, so that, by the time they came to the top of the staircase, they were carrying nothing but dead birds.

Light was waiting for them anxiously:

"Well, have you caught him?" she asked.

"Yes, yes!" said Tyltyl. "Lots of them! There are thousands! Look!"

As he spoke, he held out the dear birds to her and saw, to his dismay, that they were nothing more than lifeless corpses: their poor little wings were broken and their heads drooped sadly from their necks! The boy, in his despair, turned to his companions. Alas, they too were hugging nothing but dead birds!

Then Tyltyl threw himself sobbing into Light's arms. Once more, all his hopes were dashed to the ground.

"Do not cry, my child," said Light. "You did not catch the one that is able to live in broad daylight. . . . we shall find him yet. . . ."

"Of course, we shall find him," said Bread and Sugar, with one voice.

They were great boobies, both of them; but they wanted to console the boy. As for friend Tylô, he was so much put out that he forgot his dignity for a moment and, looking at the dead birds, exclaimed:

"Are they good to eat, I wonder?"

The party set out to walk back and sleep in the Temple of Light. It was a melancholy journey; all regretted the peace of home and felt inclined to blame Tyltyl for his want of caution. Sugar edged up to Bread and whispered in his ear:

"Don't you think, Mr. Chairman, that all this excitement is very useless?"

And Bread, who felt flattered at receiving so much attention, answered, pompously:

"Never you fear, my dear fellow, I shall put all this right. Life would be unbearable if we had to listen to all the whimsies of that little madcap! . . . To-morrow, we shall stay in bed! . . ."

They forgot that, but for the boy at whom they were sneering, they would never have been alive at all; and that, if he had suddenly told Bread that he must go back to his pan to be eaten and Sugar that he was to be cut into small lumps to sweeten Daddy Tyl's coffee and Mummy Tyl's syrups, they would have thrown themselves at their benefactor's feet and begged for mercy. In fact, they were incapable of appreciating their good luck until they were brought face to face with bad.

Poor things! The Fairy Bérylune, when making them a present of their human life, ought to have thrown in a little wisdom. They were not so much to blame. Of course, they were only following Man's example. Given the power of speaking, they jabbered; knowing how to judge, they condemned; able to feel, they complained. They had hearts which increased their sense of fear, without adding to their happiness. As to their brains, which could easily have arranged all the rest, they made so little of them that they had already grown quite rusty; and, if you could have opened their heads and looked at the works of their life inside, you would have seen the poor brains, which were their most precious possession, jumping about at every movement they made and rattling in their empty skulls like dry peas in a pod.

Fortunately, Light, thanks to her wonderful insight, knew all about their state of mind. She determined, therefore, to employ the Elements and Things no more than she was obliged to:

"They are useful," she thought, "to feed the children and amuse them on the way; but they must have no further share in the trials, because they have neither courage nor conviction."

Meanwhile, the party walked on, the road widened out and became resplendent; and, at the end, the Temple of Light stood on a crystal height, shedding its beams around. The tired Children made the Dog carry them pick-a-back by turns; and they were almost asleep when they reached the shining steps.

The Kingdom of the Future

CHAPTER V

THE KINGDOM OF THE FUTURE

TYLTYL and Mytyl woke up next morning, feeling very gay; with childish carelessness, they had forgotten their disappointment. Tyltyl was very proud of the compliments which Light had paid him: she seemed as happy as though he had brought the Blue Bird with him:

She said, with a smile, as she stroked the lad's dark curls:

"I am quite satisfied. You are such a good, brave boy that you will soon find what you are looking for."

Tyltyl did not understand the deep meaning of her words; but, for all that, he was very glad to hear them. And, besides, Light had promised him that to-day he would have nothing to fear in their new expedition. On the contrary, he would meet millions and millions of little children who would show him the most wonderful toys of which no one on earth had the least idea. She also told him that he and his little sister would travel alone with her this time and that all the others would take a rest while they were gone.

That is why, at the moment when our chapter opens, they had all met in the underground vaults of the temple. Light thought it as well to lock up the Elements and Things. She knew that, if they were left to do as they pleased, they might escape and get into mischief. It was not so very cruel of her, because the vaults of her temple are even lighter and lovelier than the upper floors of human houses; but you cannot get out without her leave. She alone has the power of widening, with a stroke of her wand, a little cleft in an emerald wall at the end of the passage, through which you go down a few crystal steps till you come to a sort of cave, all green and transparent like a forest when the sunlight sweeps through its branches.

Usually, this great hall was quite empty; but now it had sofas in it and a gold table laid with fruits and cakes and creams and delicious wines, which Light's servants had just finished setting out. Light's servants were very odd! They always made the Children laugh: with their long white satin dresses and their little black caps with a flame at the top, they looked like lighted candles. Their mistress sent them away and then told the Animals and Things to be very good and asked them if they would like some books and games to play with; they answered, with a laugh, that nothing amused them more than eating and sleeping and that they were very glad to stay where they were.

Tylô, of course, did not share this view. His heart spoke louder than his greed or his laziness; and his great dark eyes turned in entreaty on Tyltyl, who would have been only too pleased to take his faithful companion with him, if Light had not absolutely forbidden it:

"I can't help it," said the boy, giving him a kiss. "It seems that dogs are not admitted where we are going."

Suddenly, Tylô sprang up with delight: a great idea had struck him. He had not left his real, doggy life long enough to forget any part of it, especially his troubles. Which was the greatest of these? Was it not the chain? What melancholy hours Tylô had spent fastened to an iron ring! And what humiliation he endured when the wood-cutter used to take him to the village and, with unspeakable silliness, keep him on the lead in front of everybody, thus depriving him of the pleasure of greeting his friends and sniffing the smells provided for his benefit at every street-corner and in every gutter:

"Well," he said to himself, "I shall have to submit to that humiliating torture once again, to go with my little god!"

Faithful to his traditions, he had, in spite of his fine

clothes, kept his dog-collar, but not his lead. What was
to be done? He was once more in despair, when he saw
Water lying on a sofa and playing, in an absent-minded
sort of way, with her long strings of coral. He ran up to
her as prettily as he could and, after paying her a heap of
compliments, begged her to lend him her biggest necklace.
She was in a good temper and not only did what he asked,
but was kind enough to fasten the end of the coral string
to his collar. Tylô gaily went up to his master, handed
him this makeshift chain and, kneeling at his feet, said:

"Take me with you like this, my little god! Men never
say a word to a poor dog when he is on his chain!"

"Alas, even like this, you cannot come!" said Light, who
was much touched by this act of self-sacrifice; and, to cheer
him up, she told him that fate would soon provide a trial
for the Children in which his assistance would be of great
use.

As she spoke these words, she touched the emerald wall,
which opened to let her pass through with the Children.

Her chariot was waiting outside the entrance to the tem
ple. It was a lovely shell of jade, inlaid with gold. They
all three took their seats; and the two great white birds
harnessed to it at once flew off through the clouds. The
chariot travelled very fast; and they were not long on the

road, much to the regret of the Children, who were enjoying themselves and laughing like anything; but other
and even more beautiful surprises awaited them.

The clouds vanished around them; and, suddenly, they
found themselves in a dazzling azure palace. Here, all
was blue: the light, the flagstones, the columns, the vaults;
everything, down to the smallest objects, was of an intense
and fairy-like blue. There was no seeing the end of
the palace; the eyes were lost in the infinite sapphire
vistas.

"How lovely it all is!" said Tyltyl, who could not get
over his astonishment. "Goodness me, how lovely! . . .
Where are we?"

"We are in the Kingdom of the Future," said Light,
"in the midst of the children who are not yet born. As
the diamond allows us to see clearly in this region which is
hidden from men, we shall perhaps find the Blue Bird here.
. . . Look! Look at the children running up!"

From every side came bands of little children dressed
from head to foot in blue; they had beautiful dark or
golden hair and they were all exquisitely pretty. They
shouted gleefully:

"Live Children! . . . Come and look at the little Live
Children!"

"What do they call us the little Live Children for?" asked Tyltyl, of Light.

"It is because they themselves are not alive yet. They are awaiting the hour of their birth, for it is from here that all the children come who are born upon our earth. When the fathers and mothers want children, the great doors which you see over there, at the back, are opened; and the little ones go down. . . ."

"What a lot there are! What a lot there are!" cried Tyltyl.

"There are many more," said Light. "No one could count them. But go a little further: you will see other things."

Tyltyl did as he was told and elbowed his way through; but it was difficult for him to move, because a crowd of Blue Children pressed all around them. At last, by mounting on a step, our little friend was able to look over the throng of inquisitive heads and see what was happening in every part of the hall. It was most extraordinary! Tyltyl had never dreamt of anything like it! He danced with joy; and Mytyl, who was hanging on to him and standing on tiptoe so that she might see too, Mytyl clapped her hands and gave loud cries of wonder.

All around were millions of Children in blue, some playing, others walking about, others talking or thinking. Many were asleep; many also were at work; and their instruments, their tools, the machines which they were building, the plants, the flowers and the fruits which they were growing or gathering were of the same bright and heavenly blue as the general appearance of the palace. Among the Children moved tall persons also dressed in blue: they were very beautiful and looked just like angels. They came up to Light and smiled and gently pushed aside the Blue Children, who went back quietly to what they were doing, though still watching our friends with astonished eyes.

One of them, however, remained standing close to Tyltyl. He was quite small. From under his long silk sky-blue dress peeped two little pink and dimpled bare feet. His eyes stared in curiosity at the little Live Boy; and he went up to him as though in spite of himself.

"May I talk to him?" asked Tyltyl, who felt half-glad and half-frightened.

"Certainly," said Light. "You must make friends. . . . I will leave you alone; you will be more at ease by yourselves. . . ."

So saying, she went away and left the two Children face to face, shyly smiling. Suddenly, they began to talk:

"How do you do?" said Tyltyl, putting out his hand to the Child.

But the Child did not understand what that meant and stood without moving.

"What's that?" continued Tyltyl, touching the Child's blue dress.

The Child, who was absorbed in what he was looking at, did not answer, but gravely touched Tyltyl's hat with his finger:

"And that?" he lisped.

"That? . . . That's my hat," said Tyltyl. "Have you no hat?"

"No; what is it for?" asked the Child.

"It's to say How-do-you-do with," Tyltyl answered. "And then for when it's cold. . . ."

"What does that mean, when it's cold?" asked the Child.

"When you shiver like this: brrr! Brrr!" said Tyltyl. "And when you go like this with your arms," vigorously beating his arms across his chest.

"Is it cold on earth?" asked the Child.

"Yes, sometimes, in winter, when there is no fire."

"Why is there no fire? . . ."

"Because it's expensive; and it costs money to buy wood. . . ."

The Child looked at Tyltyl again as though he did not understand a word that Tyltyl was saying; and Tyltyl in his turn looked amazed:

"It's quite clear that he knows nothing of the most everyday things," thought our hero, while the child stared with no small respect at "the little Live Boy" who knew everything.

Then he asked Tyltyl what money was.

"Why, it's what you pay with!" said Tyltyl, scorning to give any further explanation.

"Oh!" said the Child, seriously.

Of course, he did not understand. How *could* he know, a little boy like that, who lived in a paradise where his least wishes were granted before he had learnt to put them into words?

"How old are you?" asked Tyltyl, continuing the conversation.

"I am going to be born soon," said the Child. "I shall be born in twelve years. . . . Is it nice to be born?"

"Oh, yes," cried Tyltyl, without thinking. "It's great fun!"

But he was very much at a loss when the little boy asked him "how he managed." His pride did not allow him to be ignorant of anything in another child's presence; and it was quite droll to see him with his hands in his breeches-pockets, his legs wide apart, his face upturned and his whole attitude that of a man who is in no hurry to reply. At last, he answered, with a shrug of the shoulders:

"Upon my word, I can't remember! It's so long ago!"

"They say it's lovely, the earth and the Live People!" remarked the Child.

"Yes, it's not bad," said Tyltyl. "There are birds and cakes and toys. . . . Some have them all; but those who have none can look at the others!"

This reflection shows us the whole character of our little friend. He was proud and inclined to be rather high-and-mighty; but he was never envious and his generous nature made up to him for his poverty by allowing him to enjoy the good fortune of others.

The two Children talked a good deal more; but it would take too long to tell you all they said, because what they said was sometimes only interesting to themselves. After a while, Light, who was watching them from a distance, hurried up to them a little anxiously: Tyltyl was crying! Big tears came rolling down his cheeks and falling on his smart coat. She understood that he was talking of his grandmother and that he could not keep back his tears at the thought of the love which he had lost. He was turning

away his head, to hide his feelings; but the inquisitive
Child kept asking him questions:

"Do the grannies die? . . . What does that mean, dying?"

"They go away one evening and do not come back."

"Has yours gone?"

"Yes," said Tyltyl. "She was very kind to me."

And, at these words, the poor little fellow began to cry
again.

The Blue Child had never seen any one cry. He lived
in a world where grief did not exist. His surprise was
great; and he exclaimed:

"What's the matter with your eyes? . . . Are they making pearls?"

To him those tears were wonderful things.

"No, it's not pearls," said Tyltyl, sheepishly.

"What is it then?"

But our poor friend would not admit what he looked
upon as a weakness. He rubbed his eyes awkwardly and
put everything down to the dazzling blue of the palace.

The puzzled Child insisted:

"What's that falling down?"

"Nothing; it's a little water," said Tyltyl, impatiently,
hoping to cut short the explanation.

But that was out of the question. The Child was very obstinate, touched Tyltyl's cheeks with his finger and asked, in a tone of curiosity:

"Does it come from the eyes? . . ."

"Yes, sometimes, when one cries."

"What does that mean, crying?" asked the Child.

"I have not been crying," said Tyltyl proudly. "It's the fault of that blue! . . . But, if I had cried, it would be the same thing. . . ."

"Do you often cry on earth? . . ."

"Not little boys, but little girls do. . . . Don't you cry here?"

"No, I don't know how. . . ."

"Well, you will learn. . . ."

At that moment, a great breath of wind made him turn his head and he saw, at a few steps away from him, a large piece of machinery which he had not noticed at first, as he was taken up with his interest in the little Child. It was a grand and magnificent thing, but I cannot tell you its name, because the inventions of the Kingdom of the Future will not be christened by Man until they reach the earth. I can only say that Tyltyl, when he looked at it, thought that the enormous azure wings that whizzed so swiftly before his eyes were like the windmills in his part of the world and that, if he ever found the Blue Bird, its wings would certainly be no more delicate, dainty or dazzling. Full of admiration, he asked his new acquaintance what they were.

"Those?" said the Child. "That's for the invention which I shall make on earth."

And, seeing Tyltyl stare with wide-open eyes, he added:

"When I am on earth, I shall have to invent the thing that gives happiness. . . . Would you like to see it? . . . It is over there, between those two columns. . . ."

Tyltyl turned round to look; but all the Children at once rushed at him, shouting:

"No, no, come and see mine! . . ."

"No, mine is much finer! . . ."

"Mine is a wonderful invention! . . ."

"Mine is made of sugar! . . ."

"His is no good! . . ."

"I'm bringing a light which nobody knows of! . . ."

And, so saying, the last Child lit himself up entirely with a most extraordinary flame.

Amid these joyous exclamations, the Live Children were dragged towards the blue workshops, where each of the little inventors set his machine going. It was a great blue whirl of disks and pulleys and straps and fly-wheels and driving-wheels and cog-wheels and all kinds of wheels,

which sent every sort of machine skimming over the ground
or shooting up to the ceiling. Other Blue Children un-
folded maps and plans, or opened great big books, or uncov-
ered azure statues, or brought enormous flowers and gigantic
fruits that seemed made of sapphires and turquoises.

Our little friends stood with their mouths wide open
and their hands clasped together: they thought themselves
in paradise. Mytyl bent over to look at a huge flower and
laughed into its cup, which covered up her head like a hood
of blue silk. A pretty Child, with dark hair and thoughtful
eyes, held it by the stalk and said, proudly:

"The flowers will all grow like that, when I am on
earth!"

"When will that be?" asked Tyltyl.

"In fifty-three years, four months and nine days."

Next came two Blue Children bending under the weight
of a pole from which was slung a bunch of grapes each
larger than a pear.

"A bunch of pears!" cried Tyltyl.

"No, they are grapes," said the Child. "They will all
be like that when I am thirty: I have found the way. . . ."

Tyltyl would have loved to taste them, but another Child
came along almost hidden under a basket which one of the
tall persons was helping him to carry. His fair-haired,

rosy face smiled through the leaves that hung over the wicker-work.

"Look!" he said. "Look at my apples. . . ."

"But those are melons!" said Tyltyl.

"No, no!" said the Child. "They are my apples! They will all be alike when I am alive! I have discovered the process! . . ."

I should never have done if I were to try and describe to my little readers all the wonderful and incredible things that appeared before our hero's eyes. But, suddenly, a loud burst of laughter rang through the hall. A Child had spoken of the King of the Nine Planets; and Tyltyl, very much puzzled and perplexed, looked on every side. All the faces, bright with laughter, were turned to some spot which Tyltyl could not see; every finger pointed in the same direction; but our friend looked in vain. They had spoken of a king! He was looking for a throne with a tall, dignified personage on it, wielding a golden sceptre.

"Over there . . . over there . . . lower down . . . behind you!" said a thousand little voices together.

"But where is the King?" Tyltyl and Mytyl repeated, greatly interested.

Then, suddenly, a louder and more serious voice sounded above the silvery murmur of the others:

"Here I am!" it said proudly.

And, at the same time, Tyltyl discovered a chubby baby which he had not yet remarked, for it was the smallest and had kept out of the way till then, sitting at the foot of a column in an attitude of indifference, seemingly rapt in contemplation. The little King was the only one who had taken no notice of the "Live Children." His beautiful, liquid eyes, eyes as blue as the palace, were pursuing endless dreams; his right hand supported his head, which was already heavy with thought; his short tunic showed his dimpled knees; and a golden crown rested on his yellow locks. When he cried, "Here I am!" the baby rose from the step on which he was sitting and tried to climb on to it at one stride; but he was still so awkward that he lost his balance and fell upon his nose. He at once picked himself up with so much dignity that nobody dared make fun of him; and, this time, he scrambled up on all fours and then, putting his legs wide apart, stood and eyed Tyltyl from top to toe.

"You're not very big!" said Tyltyl, doing his best to keep from laughing.

"I shall do great things when I am!" retorted the King, in a tone that admitted of no reply.

"And what will you do?" asked Tyltyl.

"I shall found the General Confederation of the Solar Planets," said the King, in a very pompous voice.

Our friend was so much impressed that he could not find a word to say; and the King continued:

"All the Planets will belong to it, except Uranus, Saturn and Neptune, which are too ridiculously far away."

Thereupon, he toddled off the step again and resumed his first attitude, showing that he had said all that he meant to say.

Tyltyl left him to his meditations; he was eager to know as many more of the Children as he could. He was introduced to the discoverer of a new sun, to the inventor of a new joy, to the hero who was to wipe out injustice from the earth and to the wiseacre who was to conquer Death.... There were such lots and lots of them that it would take days and days to name them all. Our friend was rather tired and was beginning to feel bored, when his attention was suddenly aroused by hearing a Child's voice calling him:

"Tyltyl! . . . Tyltyl! . . . How are you, Tyltyl, how are you? . . ."

A little Blue Child came running up from the back of the hall, pushing his way through the crowd. He was fair and slim and bright-eyed and had a great look of Mytyl.

"How do you know my name?" asked Tyltyl.

"It's not surprising," said the Blue Child, "considering that I shall be your brother!"

This time, the Live Children were absolutely amazed. What an extraordinary meeting! They must certainly tell Mummy as soon as they got back! How astonished they would be at home!

While they were making these reflections, the Child went on to explain:

"I am coming to you next year, on Palm Sunday," he said.

And he put a thousand questions to his big brother: was it comfortable at home? Was the food good? Was Daddy very severe? And Mummy?

"Oh, Mummy is so kind!" said the little ones.

And they asked him questions in their turn: what was he going to do on earth? What was he bringing?

"I am bringing three illnesses," said the little brother. "Scarlatina, whooping-cough and measles. . . ."

"Oh, that's all, is it?" cried Tyltyl.

He shook his head, with evident disappointment, while the other continued:

"After that, I shall leave you!"

"It will hardly be worth while coming!" said Tyltyl, feeling rather vexed.

"We can't pick and choose!" said the little brother, pettishly.

They would perhaps have quarrelled, without waiting till they were on earth, if they had not suddenly been parted by a swarm of Blue Children who were hurrying to meet somebody. At the same time, there was a great noise, as if thousands of invisible doors were being opened at the end of the galleries.

"What's the matter?" asked Tyltyl.

"It's Time," said one of the Blue Children. "He's going to open the doors."

And the excitement increased on every side. The Children left their machines and their labours; those who were asleep woke up; and every eye was eagerly and anxiously turned to the great opal doors at the back, while every mouth repeated the same name. The word, "Time! Time!" was heard all around; and the great mysterious noise kept on. Tyltyl was dying to know what it meant. At last, he caught a little Child by the skirt of his dress and asked him.

"Let me be," said the Child, very uneasily. "I'm in a hurry: it may be my turn to-day. . . . It is the Dawn rising. This is the hour when the Children who are to be born to-day go down to earth. . . . You shall see. . . . Time is drawing the bolts. . . ."

"Who is Time?" asked Tyltyl.

"An old man who comes to call those who are going," said another Child. "He is not so bad; but he won't listen or hear. Beg as they may, if it's not their turn, he pushes back all those who try to go. . . . Let me be! It may be my turn now!"

Light now hastened towards our little friends in a great state of alarm:

"I was looking for you," she said. "Come quick: it will never do for Time to discover you."

As she spoke these words, she threw her gold cloak around the Children and dragged them to a corner of the hall, where they could see everything, without being seen.

Tyltyl was very glad to be so well protected. He now knew that he who was about to appear possessed so great and tremendous a power that no human strength was capable of resisting him. He was at the same time a deity and an ogre; he bestowed life and he devoured it; he sped through the world so fast that you had no time to see him; he ate and ate, without stopping; he took whatever he touched. In Tyltyl's family, he had already taken

Grandad and Granny, the little brothers, the little sisters and the old blackbird! He did not mind what he took: joys and sorrows, winters and summers, all was fish that came to his net! . . .

Knowing this, our friend was astonished to see everybody in the Kingdom of the Future running so fast to meet him:

"I suppose he doesn't eat anything here," he thought.

There he was! The great doors turned slowly on their hinges. There was a distant music: it was the sounds of the earth. A red and green light penetrated into the hall; and Time appeared on the threshold. He was a tall and very thin old man, so old that his wrinkled face was all grey, like dust. His white beard came down to his knees. In one hand, he carried an enormous scythe; in the other, an hour-glass. Behind him, some way out, on a sea the colour of the Dawn, was a magnificent gold galley, with white sails.

"Are they ready whose hour has struck?" asked Time. At the sound of that voice, solemn and deep as a bronze gong, thousands of bright children's voices, like little silver bells, answered:

"Here we are! . . . Here we are! . . . Here we are! . . ."

And, in a moment, the Blue Children were crowding round the tall old man, who pushed them all back and, in a gruff voice, said:

"One at a time! . . . Once again, there are many more of you than are wanted! . . . You can't deceive me!"

Brandishing his scythe in one hand and holding out his cloak with the other, he barred the way to the rash Children who tried to slip by him. Not one of them escaped the horrid old man's watchful eye:

"It's not your turn!" he said to one. "You're to be born to-morrow! . . . Nor yours either, you've got ten years to wait. . . . A thirteenth shepherd? . . . There are only twelve wanted; there is no need for more. . . . More doctors? . . . There are too many already; they are grumbling about it on earth. . . . And where are the engineers? . . . They want an honest man; only one, as a phenomenon! . . ."

Thereupon, a poor Child, who had hung back, until then, came forward timidly, sucking his thumb. He looked pale and sad and walked with tottering footsteps; he was so wretched that even Time felt a moment's pity:

"It's you!" he exclaimed. "You seem a very poor speci·men!"

And, lifting his eyes to the sky, with a look of discouragement, he added:

"You won't live long!"

And the movement went on. Each Child, when denied, returned to his employment with a downcast air. When one of them was accepted, the others looked at him with envy. Now and then, something happened, as when the hero who was to fight against injustice refused to go. He clung to his playfellows, who called out to Time:

"He doesn't want to, Sir!"

"No, I don't want to go," cried the little fellow, with all his might. "I would rather not be born."

"And quite right too!" thought Tyltyl, who was full of common-sense and who knew what things are like on earth.

For people always get beatings which they have not deserved; and, when they have done wrong, you may be sure that the punishment will fall on one of their innocent friends.

"I wouldn't care to be in his place," said our friend to himself. "I would rather hunt for the Blue Bird, any day!"

Meanwhile, the little seeker after justice went away sobbing, frightened out of his life by Mr. Time.

The excitement was now at its height. The Children

ran all over the hall: those who were going packed up their inventions; those who were staying behind had a thousand requests to make:

"Will you write to me?"

"They say one can't!"

"Oh, try, do try!"

"Announce my idea!"

"Good-bye, Jean. . . . Good-bye, Pierre!"

"Have you forgotten nothing?"

"Don't lose your ideas!"

"Try to tell us if it's nice!"

"Enough! Enough!" roared Time, in a huge voice, shaking his big keys and his terrible scythe. "Enough! The anchor's weighed. . . ."

Then the Children climbed into the gold galley, with the beautiful white silk sails. They waved their hands again to the little friends whom they were leaving behind them; but, on seeing the earth in the distance, they cried out, gladly:

"Earth! Earth! . . . I can see it! . . ."

"How bright it is! . . ."

"How big it is! . . ."

And, at the same time, as though coming from the abyss, a song rose, a distant song of gladness and expectation.

Light, who was listening with a smile, saw the look of astonishment on Tyltyl's face and bent over him:

"It is the song of the mothers coming out to meet them," she said.

At that moment, Time, who had shut the doors, saw our friends and rushed at them angrily, shaking his scythe at them.

"Hurry!" said Light. "Hurry! Take the Blue Bird, Tyltyl, and go in front of me with Mytyl."

She put into the boy's arms a bird which she held hidden under her cloak and, all radiant, spreading her dazzling veil with her two hands, she ran on. protecting her charges from the onslaught of Time.

In this way, they passed through several turquoise and sapphire galleries. It was magnificently beautiful, but they were in the Kingdom of the Future, where Time was the great master, and they must escape from his anger which they had braved.

Mytyl was terribly frightened and Tyltyl kept nervously turning round to Light.

"Don't be afraid," she said. "I am the only person whom Time has respected since the world began. Only mind that you take care of the Blue Bird. He's gorgeous! He is quite, quite blue!"

This thought enraptured the boy. He felt the precious treasure fluttering in his arms; his hands dared not press the pretty creature's soft, warm wings; and his heart beat against its heart. This time, he held the Blue Bird! Nothing could touch it, because it was given to him by Light herself. What a triumph when he returned home! . . .

He was so bewildered by his happiness that he hardly knew where he was going; his joy rang a victorious peal in his head that made him feel giddy; he was mad with pride; and this, worse luck, made him lose his coolness and his presence of mind! They were just about to cross the threshold of the palace, when a gust of wind swept through the entrance-hall, lifting up Light's veil and at last revealing the two Children to the eyes of Time, who was still pursuing them. With a roar of rage, he darted his scythe at Tyltyl, who cried out. Light warded off the blow; and the door of the palace closed behind them with a thud. They were saved! . . . But alas, Tyltyl, taken by surprise, had opened his arms and now, through his tears, saw the Bird of the Future soaring above their heads, mingling with the azure sky its dream-wings so blue, so light and so transparent that soon the boy could make out nothing more. . . .

In the Temple of Light

CHAPTER VI

IN THE TEMPLE OF LIGHT

TYLTYL had enjoyed himself thoroughly in the Kingdom
of the Future. He had seen many wonderful things and
thousands of little playfellows and then, without taking the
least pains or trouble, had found the Blue Bird in his arms
in the most miraculous way. He had never pictured anything more beautiful, more blue or brilliant; and he still
felt it fluttering against his heart and kept hugging his arms
to his breast as though the Blue Bird were there.

Alas, it had vanished like a dream!

He was thinking sadly of this latest disappointment as
he walked hand-in-hand with Light. They were back in
the Temple and were going to the vaults where the Animals
and Things had been shut up. What a sight met their eyes!
The wretches had eaten and drunk such a lot that they were
lying on the floor quite tipsy! Tylô himself had lost all
his dignity. He had rolled under the table and was snoring like a porpoise. His instinct remained; and the sound
of the door made him prick up his ears. He opened one

eye, but his sight was troubled by all that he had had to drink and he did not know his little master when he saw him. He dragged himself to his feet with a great effort, turned round several times and then dropped on the floor again with a grunt of satisfaction.

Bread and the others were as bad; and the only exception was the Cat, who was sitting up prettily on a marble and gold bench and seemed in full possession of her senses. She sprang nimbly to the ground and stepped up to Tyltyl with a smile:

"I have been longing to see you," she said, "for I have been very unhappy among all these vulgar people. They first drank all the wine and then started shouting and singing and dancing, quarrelling and fighting and making such a noise that I was very glad when, at last, they fell into a tipsy sleep."

The children praised her warmly for her good behaviour. As a matter of fact, there was no great merit in this, for she could not stand anything stronger than milk; but we are seldom rewarded when by rights we ought to be and sometimes are when we have not deserved it.

After fondly kissing the children, Tylette asked a favour of Light:

"I have had such a wretched time," she whined. "Let

me go out for a little while; it will do me good to be alone."

Light gave her consent without suspecting anything; and the Cat at once draped her cloak round her, put her hat straight, pulled up her soft grey boots over her knees, opened the door and ran and bounded out into the forest. We shall know, a little later, where treacherous Tylette was going so gaily and what was the horrid plot which she was mysteriously concocting.

As on the other days, the Children had their dinner with Light in a large room all encrusted with diamonds. The servants bustled around them smiling and brought delicious dishes and cakes.

After dinner, our little friends began to yawn. They felt sleepy very early, after all their adventures; and, Light —ever kind and thoughtful—made them live as they were accustomed to on earth. So as not to injure their health by altering their habits, she had set up their little beds in a part of the temple where the darkness would seem like night to them.

They went through any number of rooms to reach their bedroom. They had first to pass all the lights known to Man and then those which Man did not yet know.

There were great sumptuous apartments in splendid marble, lit up by rays so white and strong that the children were quite dazzled.

"That is the Light of the Rich," said Light to Tyltyl. "You see how dangerous it is. People run the risk of going blind when they live too much in its rays, which leave no room for soft and kindly shade."

And she hurried them on so that they might rest their eyes in the gentle Light of the Poor. Here, the Children suddenly felt as if they were in their parents' cottage, where everything was so humble and peaceful. The faint light was very pure and clear, but always flickering and ready to go out at the least breath.

Next they came to the beautiful Light of the Poets, which they liked immensely, for it had all the colours of the rainbow; and, when you passed through it, you saw lovely pictures, lovely flowers and lovely toys which you were unable to take hold of. Laughing merrily, the children ran after birds and butterflies, but everything faded away as soon as it was touched.

"Well, I never!" said Tyltyl, as he came panting back to Light. "This beats everything! I can't understand it!"

"You will understand later," she replied, "and, if you understand it properly, you will be among the very few human beings who know the Blue Bird when they see him."

After leaving the region of the Poets, our friends reached the Light of the Learned, which lies on the borders of the known and the unknown lights:

"Let's get on," said Tyltyl. "This is boring."

To tell the truth, he was a little bit frightened, for they were in a long row of cold and forbidding arches, which were streaked at every moment by dazzling lightning-flashes; and, at each flash, you saw out-of-the-way things that had no name as yet.

After these arches, they came to the Lights Unknown to Man; and Tyltyl, in spite of the sleep that pressed upon his eyelids, could not help admiring the hall with its violet columns and the gallery with its red rays. And the violet of the columns was such a dark violet and the red of the rays such a pale red that it was hardly possible to see either of them.

At last, they arrived at the room of smooth, unflecked Black Light, which men call Darkness because their eyes are not yet able to make it out. And here the Children fell asleep without delay on two soft beds of clouds.

The Graveyard

CHAPTER VII

THE GRAVEYARD

WHEN the Children were not going on an expedition, they played about in the Realms of Light; and this was a great treat for them, for the gardens and the country around the temple were as wonderful as the halls and galleries of silver and gold.

The leaves of some of the plants were so broad and strong that they were able to lie down on them; and, when a breath of wind stirred the leaves, the Children swung as in a hammock. It was always summer there and never a moment was darkened by the night; but the hours were known by their different colours; there were pink, white, blue, lilac, green and yellow hours; and, according to their hues, the flowers, the fruits, the birds, the butterflies and the scents changed, causing Tyltyl and Mytyl a perpetual surprise. They had all the toys that they could wish for. When they were tired of playing, they stretched themselves out on the backs of the lizards, which were as long and wide as little boats, and quickly, quickly raced round the garden-

125

paths, over the sand which was as white and as good to eat as sugar. When they were thirsty, Water shook her tresses into the cup of the enormous flowers; and the Children drank straight out of the lilies, tulips and convolvuluses. If they were hungry, they picked radiant fruits which revealed the taste of Light to them and which had juice that shone like the rays of the sun.

There was also, in a clump of bushes, a white marble pond which possessed a magic power: its clear waters reflected not the faces, but the souls of those who looked into it.

"It's a ridiculous invention," said the Cat, who steadily refused to go near the pond.

You, my dear little readers, who know her thoughts as well as I do, will not be surprised at her refusal. And you will also understand why our faithful Tylô was not afraid to go and quench his thirst there: he need not fear to reveal his thoughts, for he was the only creature whose soul never altered. The dear Dog had no feelings but those of love and kindness and devotion.

When Tyltyl bent over the magic mirror, he almost always saw the picture of a splendid Blue Bird, for the constant wish to find him filled his mind entirely. Then he would run to Light and entreat her:

"Tell me where he is! . . . You know everything: tell me where to find him!"

But she replied, in a tone of mystery:

"I cannot tell you anything. You must find him for yourself." And, kissing him, she added, "Cheer up; you are getting nearer to him at each trial."

Now there came a day on which she said to him:

"I have received a message from the Fairy Bérylune telling me that the Blue Bird is probably hidden in the graveyard. . . . It appears that one of the Dead in the graveyard is keeping him in his tomb. . . ."

"What shall we do?" asked Tyltyl.

"It is very simple: at midnight you will turn the diamond and you shall see the Dead come out of the ground."

At these words, Milk, Water, Bread and Sugar began to yell and scream and chatter their teeth like anything.

"Don't mind them," said Light to Tyltyl, in a whisper. "They are afraid of the Dead."

"I'm not afraid of them!" said Fire, frisking about. "Time was when I used to burn them; that was much more amusing than nowadays."

"Oh, I feel I am going to turn," wailed Milk.

"I'm not afraid," said the Dog, trembling in every limb,

"but if you run away . . . I shall run away too . . . and with the greatest pleasure . . ."

The Cat sat pulling at her whiskers:

"I know what's what," she said, in her usual mysterious way.

"Be quiet," said Light. "The Fairy gave strict orders, You are all to stay with me, at the gate of the graveyard; the Children are to go in alone."

Tyltyl felt anything but pleased. He asked:

"Aren't you coming with us?"

"No," said Light. "The time for that has not arrived. Light cannot yet enter among the Dead. Besides, there is nothing to fear. I shall not be far away; and those who love me and whom I love always find me again . . ."

She had not finished speaking, when everything around the Children changed. The wonderful temple, the dazzling flowers, the splendid gardens vanished to make way for a poor little country cemetery, which lay in the soft moonlight. Near the Children were a number of graves, grassy mounds, wooden crosses and tombstones. Tyltyl and Mytyl were seized with terror and hugged each other:

"I am frightened!" said Mytyl.

"I am never frightened," stammered Tyltyl, who was shaking with fear, but did not like to say so.

"I say," asked Mytyl, "are the Dead wicked?"

"Why, no," said Tyltyl, "they're not alive! . . ."

"Have you ever seen one?"

"Yes, once, long ago, when I was very young . . ."

"What was it like?"

"Quite white, very still and very cold; and it didn't talk . . ."

"Are we going to see them?"

Tyltyl shuddered at this question and made an unsuccess· ful effort to steady his voice as he answered:

"Why, of course, Light said so!"

"Where are the Dead?" asked Mytyl.

Tyltyl cast a frightened look around him, for the Children had not dared to stir since they were alone:

"The Dead are here," he said, "under the grass or under those big stones."

"Are those the doors of their houses?" asked Mytyl, pointing to the tombstones.

"Yes."

"Do they go out when it's fine?"

"They can only go out at night."

"Why?"

"Because they are in their nightshirts."

"Do they go out also when it rains?"

"When it rains, they stay at home."

"Is it nice in their homes?"

"They say it's very cramped."

"Have they any little children?"

"Why, yes, they have all those who die."

"And what do they live on?"

Tyltyl stopped to think, before answering. As Mytyl's big brother, he felt it his duty to know everything; but her questions often puzzled him. Then he reflected that, as the Dead live under ground, they can hardly eat anything that is above it; and so he answered very positively:

"They eat roots!"

Mytyl was quite satisfied and returned to the great question that was occupying her little mind:

"Shall we see them?" she asked.

"Of course," said Tyltyl, "we see everything when I turn the diamond."

"And what will they say?"

Tyltyl began to grow impatient:

"They will say nothing, as they don't talk."

"Why don't they talk?" asked Mytyl.

"Because they have nothing to say," said Tyltyl, more cross and perplexed than ever.

"Why have they nothing to say?"

This time, the little big brother lost all patience. He shrugged his shoulders, gave Mytyl a push and shouted angrily:

"You're a nuisance! . . ."

Mytyl was greatly upset and confused. She sucked her thumb and resolved to hold her tongue for ever after, as she had been so badly treated! But a breath of wind made the leaves of the trees whisper and suddenly recalled the Children to their fears and their sense of loneliness. They hugged each other tight and began to talk again, so as not to hear the horrible silence:

"When will you turn the diamond?" asked Mytyl.

"You heard Light say that I was to wait until midnight, because that disturbs them less; it is when they come out to take the air. , . ."

"Isn't it midnight yet . . ."

Tyltyl turned round, saw the church clock and hardly had the strength to answer, for the hands were just upon the hour:

"Listen," he stammered, "listen . . . It is just going to strike . . . There! . . . Do you hear? . . ."

And the clock struck twelve.

Then Mytyl, frightened out of her life, began to stamp her feet and utter piercing screams:

"I want to go away! . . . I want to go away! . . ."

Tyltyl, though stiff with fright, was able to say:

"Not now . . . I am going to turn the diamond . . ."

"No, no, no!" cried Mytyl. "I am so frightened, little brother! . . . Don't do it! . . . I want to go away! . . ."

Tyltyl vainly tried to lift his hand: he could not reach the diamond with Mytyl clinging to him, hanging with all her weight on her brother's arm and screaming at the top of her voice:

"I don't want to see the Dead! . . . They will be awful! . . . I can't possibly! . . . I am much too frightened! . . ."

Poor Tyltyl was quite as much terrified as Mytyl, but at each trial, his will and courage were becoming greater; he was learning to master himself; and nothing could induce him to fail in his mission. The eleventh stroke rang out.

"The hour is passing!" he exclaimed. "It is time!"

And releasing himself resolutely from Mytyl's arms, he turned the diamond . . .

A moment of terrible silence followed for the poor little children. Then they saw the crosses totter, the mounds open, the slabs rise up . . .

Mytyl hid her face against Tyltyl's chest:

"They're coming out!" she cried. "They're there! . . . They're there! . . ."

The agony was more than the plucky little fellow could endure. He shut his eyes and only kept himself from fainting by leaning against a tree beside him. He remained like that for a minute that seemed to him like a century, not daring to move, not daring to breathe. Then he heard birds singing; a warm and scented breeze fanned his face; and, on his hands, on his neck, he felt the soft heat of the balmy summer sun. Now quite reassured, but unable to believe in so great a miracle, he opened his eyes and at once began to shout with happiness and admiration.

From all the open tombs came thousands of splendid flowers. They spread everywhere, on the paths, on the trees, on the grass; and they went up and up until it seemed that they would touch the sky. They were great full-blown roses, showing their hearts, wonderful golden hearts from which came the hot, bright rays which had wrapped Tyltyl in that summer warmth. Round the roses, birds sang and bees buzzed gaily.

"I can't believe it! It's not possible!" said Tyltyl. "What has become of the tombs and the stone crosses?"

Dazzled and bewildered, the two children walked hand in hand through the graveyard, of which not a trace remained, for there was nothing but a wonderful garden on every side. They were as glad and happy as could be, after

their terrible fright.   They had thought that ugly skeletons
would rise from the earth and run after them, pulling horrid
faces; they had imagined all sorts of awful things.   And
now, in the presence of the truth, they saw that all that
they had been told was a great big story and that Death does
not exist.   They saw that there are no Dead and that Life
goes on always, always, but under fresh forms.   The fading
rose sheds its pollen, which gives birth to other roses, and
its scattered petals scent the air.   The fruits come when
the blossoms fall from the trees; and the dingy, hairy cater-
pillar turns into a brilliant butterfly.   Nothing perishes
. . . there are only changes . . .

Beautiful birds circled all round Tyltyl and Mytyl.
There were no blue ones among them, but the two Children
were so glad of their discovery that they asked for nothing
more.   Astonished and delighted, they kept on repeating:

"There are no Dead! . . . There are no Dead! . . ."

The Forest

CHAPTER VIII

THE FOREST

As soon as Tyltyl and Mytyl were in bed, Light kissed them and faded away at once, so as not to disturb their sleep with the rays that always streamed from her beautiful self.

It must have been about midnight, when Tyltyl, who was dreaming of the little Blue Children, felt a soft velvet paw pass to and fro over his face. He was surprised and sat up in bed in a bit of a fright; but he was soon reassured when he saw his friend Tylette's glowing eyes glittering in the dark.

"Hush!" said the Cat in his ear. "Hush! Don't wake anybody. If we can arrange to slip out without being seen, we shall catch the Blue Bird to-night. I have risked my life, O my dearest master, in preparing a plan which will certainly lead us to victory!"

"But," said the boy, kissing Tylette, "Light would be so glad to help us . . . and besides I should be ashamed to disobey her . . ."

"If you tell her," said the Cat, sharply, "all is lost, believe me.   Do as I say; and the day is ours."

As she spoke these words, she hastened to dress him and also Mytyl, who had heard a noise and was asking to go with them.

"You don't understand," groaned Tyltyl.   "You are too small: you don't know what a wicked thing we are do-ing . . ."

But the treacherous Cat answered all his arguments, say-ing that the reason why he had not found the Blue Bird so far was just the fault of Light, who always brought bright-ness with her.   Let the Children only go hunting by them-selves, in the dark, and they would soon find all the Blue Birds that make men's happiness.   The traitress displayed such cleverness that, before long, Tyltyl's disobedience be-came a very fine thing in his own eyes.   Each of Tylette's words provided a good excuse for his action or adorned it with a generous thought.   He was too weak to set his will against trickery, allowed himself to be persuaded and walked out of the temple with a firm and cheerful step. Poor little fellow: if he could only have foreseen the terrible trap that awaited him!

Our three companions set out across the fields in the white light of the moon.   The Cat seemed greatly excited, did nothing but talk and went so fast that the children were hardly able to keep up with her:

"This time," she declared, "we shall have the Blue Bird, I am sure of it! I asked all the Trees in the very oldest forest; they know him, because he hides among them. Then, in order to have everybody there, I sent the Rabbit to beat the assembly and convoke the principal Animals in the country."

They reached the edge of the dark forest in an hour's time. Then, at a turn in the road, they saw, in the distance, some one who seemed to be hurrying towards them. Tylette arched her back: she felt that it was her inveterate enemy. She quivered with rage: was he once more going to thwart her plans? Had he guessed her secret? Was he coming, at the last moment, to save the Children's lives?

She leant over to Tyltyl and whispered to him, in her most honeyed voice:

"I am sorry to say it is our worthy friend the Dog. It is a thousand pities, because his presence will make us fail in our object. He is on the worst of terms with everybody, even the Trees. Do tell him to go back!"

"Go away, you ugly thing!" said Tyltyl, shaking his fist at the Dog.

Dear old faithful Tylô, who had come because he suspected the Cat's plans, was much hurt by these hard words. He was ready to cry, was still out of breath from running and could think of nothing to say.

"Go away, I tell you!" said Tyltyl again. "We don't want you here and there's an end of it . . . You're a nui‑sance, there! . . ."

The Dog was an obedient animal and, at any other time, he would have gone; but his affection told him what a serious business it was and he stood stock still.

"Do you allow this disobedience?" said the Cat to Tyltyl, in a whisper. "Hit him with your stick."

Tyltyl beat the Dog, as the Cat suggested:

"There, that will teach you to be more obedient!" he said.

The poor Dog howled at receiving the blows; but there was no limit to his self-sacrifice. He went up to his young master pluckily and, taking him in his arms, cried:

"I must kiss you now you've beaten me!"

Tyltyl, who was a good-hearted little fellow, did not know what to do; and the Cat swore between her teeth like a wild beast. Fortunately, dear little Mytyl interfered on our friend's behalf:

"No, no; I want him to stay," she pleaded. "I'm fright‑ened when Tylô's not there."

Time was short and they had to come to a decision.

"I'll find some other way to get rid of the idiot!" thought the Cat. And, turning to the Dog, she said, in her most gracious manner, "We shall be *so* pleased if you will join us!"

As they entered the great forest, the Children stuck close together, with the Cat and the Dog on either side of them. They were awed by the silence and the darkness and they felt much relieved when the Cat exclaimed:

"Here we are! Turn the diamond!"

Then the light spread around them and showed them a wonderful sight. They were standing in the middle of a large round space in the heart of the forest, where all the old, old Trees seemed to reach up to the sky. Wide avenues formed a white star amidst the dark green of the wood. Everything was peaceful and still; but suddenly a strange shiver ran through the foliage; the branches moved and stretched like human arms; the roots raised the earth that covered them, came together, took the shapes of legs and feet and stood on the ground; a tremendous crash rang through the air; the trunks of the Trees burst open and each of them let out its soul, which made its appearance like a funny human figure.

Some stepped slowly from their trunks; others came out with a jump; and all of them gathered inquisitively round our friends.

The talkative Poplar began to chatter like a magpie:

"Little Men! We shall be able to talk to them! We have done with silence! . . . Where do they come from? . . . Who are they?"

And so he rattled on.

The Lime-tree, who was a jolly, fat fellow, came up calmly, smoking his pipe; the conceited and dandified Chestnut-tree screwed his glass into his eye to stare at the Children. He wore a coat of green silk embroidered with pink and white flowers. He thought the little ones too poor-looking and turned away in derision.

"He thinks he's everybody, since he has taken to living in town! He despises us!" sneered the Poplar, who was jealous of him.

"Oh, dear, oh, dear!" wept the Willow, a wretched little stunted fellow, who came clattering along in a pair of wooden shoes too big for him. "They have come to cut off my head and arms for firewood!"

Tyltyl could not believe his eyes. He never stopped asking the Cat questions:

"Who's this? . . . Who's that? . . ."

And Tylette introduced the soul of each Tree to him.

There was the Elm, who was a sort of short-winded, paunchy, crabby gnome; the Beech, an elegant, sprightly person; the Birch, who looked like the ghosts in the Palace of Night, with his white flowing garments and his restless gestures. The tallest figure was the Fir-tree: Tyltyl found it very difficult to see his face perched right at the top of his long, thin body; but he looked gentle and sad, whereas the Cypress, who stood near him, dressed all in black, frightened Tyltyl terribly.

However, so far nothing very dreadful had happened. The Trees, delighted at being able to talk, were all chattering together; and our young friend was simply going to ask them where the Blue Bird was hidden, when, all of a sudden, silence reigned. The Trees bowed respectfully and stood aside to make way for an immensely old Tree, dressed in a long gown embroidered with moss and lichen. He leant with one hand on a stick and with the other on a young Oak Sapling who acted as his guide, for the Old Oak was blind. His long white beard streamed in the wind.

"It's the King!" said Tyltyl to himself, when he saw his mistletoe crown. "I will ask him the secret of the forest."

And he was just going up to him, when he stopped, seized with surprise and joy: there sat the Blue Bird before him, perched on the old Oak's shoulder.

"He has the Blue Bird!" cried the boy, gleefully. "Quick! Quick! Give him to me!"

"Silence! Hold your tongue!" said the greatly shocked Trees.

"Take off your hat, Tyltyl," said the Cat. "It's the Oak!"

The poor Child at once obeyed with a smile; he did not understand the danger that threatened him and he did not hesitate to answer, "Yes, Sir," when the Oak asked him if he was Tyl the woodcutter's son.

Then the Oak, trembling with rage, began to lay a terrible charge against Daddy Tyl:

"In my family alone," he said, "your father has put to death six hundred of my sons, four hundred and seventy-five uncles and aunts, twelve hundred cousins of both sexes, three hundred and eighty daughters-in-law and twelve thousand great-grandsons!"

No doubt his anger made him exaggerate a little; but Tyltyl listened without protest and said, very politely:

"I beg your pardon, Sir, for disturbing you . . . The Cat said that you would tell us where the Blue Bird was."

The Oak was too old not to know all there was to know about Men and Animals. He smiled in his beard when he guessed the trap laid by the Cat and he felt very glad at it, for he had long wished to revenge the whole forest for the slavery to which Man had subjected it.

"It's for the Fairy Bérylune's little girl, who is very ill," the boy continued.

"Enough!" said the Oak, silencing him. "I do not hear the Animals . . . Where are they? . . . All this concerns them as much as us. . . . We, the Trees, must not assume the responsibility alone for the grave measures that have become necessary."

"Here they come!" said the Fir-tree, looking over the top of the other Trees. "They are following the Rabbit . . . I can see the souls of the Horse, the Bull, the Ox, the Cow, the Wolf, the Sheep, the Pig, the Goat, the Ass and the Bear. . . ."

All the Animals now arrived. They walked on their hind-legs and were dressed like human beings. They solemnly took up their positions in a circle among the Trees, all except the frivolous Goat, who began to skip down the avenues, and the Pig, who hoped to find some glorious truffles among the roots that had newly left the ground.

"Are all here present?" asked the Oak.

"The Hen could not leave her eggs," said the Rabbit, "the Hare was out for a run, the Stag has pains in his horns and his corns, the Fox is ill—here is the doctor's certificate— the Goose did not understand and the Turkey flew into a passion. . . ."

"Look!" whispered Tyltyl to Mytyl. "Aren't they funny? They are just like the rich children's fine toys in the windows at Christmas-time."

The Rabbit especially made them laugh, with his cocked hat over his big ears, his blue, embroidered coat and his drum slung in front of him.

Meanwhile, the Oak was explaining the situation to his brothers the Trees and to the Animals. Treacherous Tylette had been quite right in reckoning on their hatred.

"The child you see before you," said the Oak, "thanks to a talisman stolen from the powers of Earth, is able to take possession of our Blue Bird and thus to snatch from us the secret which we have kept since the origin of life. . . . Now we know enough of Man to entertain no doubt as to the fate which he reserves for us, once he is in possession of this secret. . . . Any hesitation would be both foolish and criminal . . . It is a serious moment; the child must be done away with before it is too late. . . ."

"What is he saying?" asked Tyltyl, who could not make out what the old Tree was driving at.

The Dog was prowling round the Oak and now showed his fangs:

"Do you see my teeth, you old cripple?" he growled.

"He is insulting the Oak!" said the Beech indignantly.

"Drive him out!" shouted the Oak, angrily. "He's a traitor!"

"What did I tell you?" whispered the Cat to Tyltyl. "I will arrange things . . . But send him away."

"Will you be off!" said Tyltyl to the Dog.

"Do let me worry the gouty old beggar's moss slippers!" begged Tylô.

Tyltyl tried in vain to prevent him. The rage of Tylô, who understood the danger, knew no bounds; and he would have succeeded in saving his master, if the Cat had not thought of calling in the Ivy, who till then had kept his distance. The Dog pranced about like a madman, abusing everybody. He railed at the Ivy:

"Come on, if you dare, you old ball of twine, you!"

The onlookers growled; the Oak was pale with fury at seeing his authority denied; the Trees and the Animals were indignant, but, as they were cowards, not one of them dared protest; and the Dog would have settled all of them, if he had gone on with his rebellion. But Tyltyl threatened him harshly; and, suddenly yielding to his docile instincts, Tylô lay down at his master's feet. Thus it is that our finest virtues are treated as faults, when we exercise them without discrimination.

From that moment, the Children were lost. The Ivy

gagged and bound the poor Dog, who was then taken behind the Chestnut-tree and tied to his biggest root.

"Now," cried the Oak, in a voice of thunder, "we can take counsel quietly . . . This is the first time that it is given us to judge Man! I do not think that, after the monstrous injustice which we have suffered, there can remain the least doubt as to the sentence that awaits him. . . ."

One cry rang from every throat:

"Death! Death! Death!"

The poor Children did not at first understand their doom, for the Trees and Animals, who were more accustomed to talking their own special language, did not speak very distinctly; and, besides, the innocent Children could never imagine such cruelty!

"What is the matter with them?" asked the boy. "Are they displeased?"

"Don't be alarmed," said the Cat. "They are a little annoyed because Spring is late. . . ."

And she went on talking into Tyltyl's ear, to divert his attention from what was happening.

While the trusting lad was listening to her fibs, the others were discussing which form of execution would be the most practical and the least dangerous. The Bull suggested a good butt with the horns; the Beech offered his highest branch to hang the little Children on; and the Ivy was already preparing a slip-knot! The Fir-tree was willing to give the four planks for the coffin and the Cypress the perpetual grant of a tomb.

"By far the simplest way," whispered the Willow, "would be to drown them in one of my rivers."

And the Pig grunted between his teeth:

"In my opinion, the great thing would be to eat the little girl. . . . She ought to be very tender. . . ."

"Silence!" roared the Oak. "What we have to decide is which of us shall have the honour of striking the first blow!"

"That honour falls to you, our King!" said the Fir-tree.

"Alas, I am too old!" replied the Oak. "I am blind and infirm! To you, my evergreen brother, be the glory, in my place, of striking the decisive blow that shall set us free."

But the Fir-tree declined the honour on the pretext that he was already to have the pleasure of burying the two victims and that he was afraid of rousing jealousy. He suggested the Beech, as owning the best club.

"It is out of the question," said the Beech. "You know I am worm-eaten! Ask the Elm and the Cypress."

Thereupon the Elm began to moan and groan: a mole had twisted his great toe the night before and he could hardly stand upright; and the Cypress excused himself and so did the Poplar, who declared that he was ill and shivering with fever.   Then the Oak's indignation flared up:

"You are afraid of Man!" he exclaimed.   "Even those unprotected and unarmed little Children inspire you with terror! . . . Well, I shall go forth alone, old and shaky and blind as I am, against the hereditary enemy! . . . Where is he? . . ."

And groping his way with his stick, he moved towards Tyltyl, growling as he went.

Our poor little friend had been very much afraid during the last few minutes.   The Cat had left him suddenly, saying that she wanted to smooth down the excitement, and had not come back.   Mytyl nestled trembling against him; and he felt very lonely, very unhappy among those dreadful people whose anger he was beginning to notice.   When he saw the Oak marching on him with a threatening air, he drew his pocket-knife and defied him like a man:

"Is it me he's after, that old one, with his big stick?" he cried.

But, at the sight of the knife, Man's irresistible weapon, all the Trees shook with fright and rushed at the Oak to hold him back.   There was a struggle; and the old King, conquered by the weight of years, threw away his stick:

"Shame on us!" he shouted. "Shame on us! Let the Animals deliver us! . . ."

The Animals were only waiting for this! All wanted to be revenged together. Fortunately, their very eagerness caused a scrimmage which delayed the murder of the dear little ones.

Mytyl uttered piercing screams.

"Don't be afraid," said Tyltyl, doing his best to protect her. "I have my knife."

"The little chap means to die game!" said the Cock.

"That's the one I shall eat first," said the Pig, eyeing Mytyl greedily.

"What have I done to all of you?" asked Tyltyl.

"Nothing at all, my little man," said the Sheep. "Eaten my little brother, my two sisters, my three uncles, my aunt, my grandpapa and my grandmamma. . . . Wait, wait, when you're down, you shall see that I have teeth also. . ."

And so the Sheep, the Ass and the Horse, who were the greatest cowards, waited for the little fellow to be knocked down before they dared take their share in the spoil.

While they were talking, the Wolf and the Bear treacherously attacked Tyltyl from behind and pushed him over. It was an awful moment. All the Animals, seeing him on the ground, tried to get at him. The boy raised himself to one knee and brandished his knife. Mytyl uttered yells of distress; and, to crown all, it suddenly became dark.

Tyltyl called wildly for assistance:

"Help! Help! . . . Tylô! Tylô! . . . To the rescue! . . . Where is Tylette? . . . Come! Come! . . ."

The Cat's voice was heard in the distance, where she was craftily keeping out of sight:

"I can't come!" she whined. "I'm wounded!"

All this time, plucky little Tyltyl was defending himself as best he could, but he was alone against all of them, felt that he was going to be killed and, in a faltering voice, cried once more:

"Help! . . . Tylô! Tylô! . . . I can't hold out! . . . There are too many of them! . . . The Bear! . . . The Pig! The Wolf! The Ass! The Fir-tree! The Beech! . . . Tylô! Tylô! Tylô! . . ."

Then the Dog came leaping along, dragging his broken bonds and elbowing his way through the Trees and Animals and flung himself before his master, whom he defended furiously:

"Here, my little god! Don't be afraid! Have at them! I know how to use my teeth!"

All the Trees and Animals raised a loud outcry:

"Renegade! . . . Idiot! . . . Traitor! . . . Felon! . . .

Simpleton! . . . Sneak! . . . Leave him! . . . He's a dead man! . . . Come over to us! . . ."

The Dog fought on:

"Never! Never! . . . I alone against all of you! . . . Never! Never! . . . True to the gods, to the best, to the greatest! . . . Take care, my little master, here's the Bear! . . . Look out for the Bull!"

Tyltyl vainly tried to defend himself:

"I'm done for, Tylô! It was a blow from the Elm! My hand's bleeding!" And he dropped to the ground. "No, I can hold out no longer!"

"They are coming!" said the Dog. "I hear somebody! . . . We are saved! It is Light! . . . Saved! Saved! . . . See, they're afraid, they're retreating! . . . Saved, my little king! . . ."

And, sure enough, Light was coming towards them; and with her the dawn rose over the forest, which became light as day.

"What is it? . . . What has happened?" she asked, quite alarmed at the sight of the little ones and their dear Tylô covered with wounds and bruises. "Why, my poor boy, didn't you know? Turn the diamond quickly!"

Tyltyl hastened to obey; and immediately the souls of all the Trees rushed back into their trunks, which closed upon them. The souls of the Animals also disappeared; and there was nothing to be seen but a cow and a sheep browsing peacefully in the distance. The forest became harmless once more; and Tyltyl looked around him in amazement:

"No matter," he said, "but for the Dog . . . and if I hadn't had my knife! . . ."

Light thought that he had been punished enough and did not scold him. Besides, she was very much upset by the horrible danger which he had run.

Tyltyl, Mytyl and the Dog, glad to meet again safe and sound, exchanged wild kisses. They laughingly counted their wounds, which were not very serious.

Tylette was the only one to make a fuss:

"The Dog's broken my paw!" she mewed.

Tylô felt as if he could have made a mouthful of her:

"Never mind!" he said. "It'll keep!"

"Leave her alone, will you, you ugly beast?" said Mytyl.

Our friends went back to the Temple of Light to rest after their adventure. Tyltyl, repenting of his disobedience, dared not even mention the Blue Bird of which he had caught a glimpse; and Light said to the Children, gently:

"Let this teach you, dears, that Man is all alone against all in this world. Never forget that."

The Leave-Taking

CHAPTER IX

THE LEAVE-TAKING

WEEKS and months had passed since the children's departure on their journey; and the hour of separation was at hand. Light had been very sad lately; she had counted the days in sorrow, without a word to the Animals and Things, who had no idea of the misfortune that threatened them.

On the day when we see them for the last time, they were all out in the gardens of the temple. Light stood watching them from a marble terrace, with Tyltyl and Mytyl sleeping by her side. Much had happened in the past twelve months; but the life of the Animals and Things, which had no intelligence to guide it, had made no progress: on the contrary! Bread had eaten so much that he was now not able to walk: Milk, devoted as ever, dragged him along in a Bath chair. Fire's nasty temper had made him quarrel with everybody and he had become very lonely and unhappy in consequence. Water, who had no will of her own, had ended by yielding to Sugar's sweet entreaties: they were now married; and Sugar presented a most piteous

157

sight. The poor fellow was reduced to a shadow of his
former self, shrank visibly day by day and was sillier than
ever, while Water, in marrying, had lost her principal
charm, her simplicity. The Cat had remained the liar that
she always was; and our dear friend Tylô had never been
able to overcome his hatred for her.

"Poor things!" thought Light, with a sigh. "They have
not gained much by receiving the benefit of life! They
have travelled and seen nothing of all the wonders that surrounded them in my peaceful temple; they were either quarrelling with one another or over-eating themselves until
they fell ill. They were too foolish to enjoy their happiness and they will recognize it for the first time presently,
when they are about to lose it. . . ."

At that moment, a pretty dove, with silver wings, alighted
on her knees. It wore an emerald collar round its neck, with
a note fastened to the clasp. The dove was the Fairy Bérylune's messenger. Light opened the letter and read these
few words:

"Remember that the year is over."

Then Light stood up, waved her wand and everything
disappeared from sight.

A few seconds later, the whole company were gathered together outside a high wall with a small door in it. The first rays of the dawn were gilding the tree-tops. Tyltyl and Mytyl, whom Light was fondly supporting with her arms, woke up, rubbed their eyes and looked around them in astonishment.

"What?" said Light to Tyltyl. "Don't you know that wall and that little door?"

The sleepy boy shook his head: he remembered nothing. Then Light assisted his memory:

"The wall," she said, "surrounds a house which we left one evening just a year ago to-day. . . ."

"Just a year ago? . . . Why, then . . ." And, clapping his hands with glee, Tyltyl ran to the door. "We must be near Mummy! . . . I want to kiss her at once, at once, at once!"

But Light stopped him. It was too early, she said: Mummy and Daddy were still asleep and he must not wake them with a start.

"Besides," she added, "the door will not open till the hour strikes."

"What hour?" asked the boy.

"The hour of separation," Light answered, sadly.

"What!" said Tyltyl, in great distress. "Are you leav‑ing us?"

"I must," said Light. "The year is past. The Fairy will come back and ask you for the Blue Bird."

"But I haven't got the Blue Bird!" cried Tyltyl. "The one of the Land of Memory turned quite black, the one of the Future flew away, the Night's are dead, those in the Graveyard were not blue and I could not catch the one in the Forest! . . . Will the Fairy be angry? . . . What will she say? . . ."

"Never mind, dear," said Light. "You did your best. And, though you did not find the Blue Bird, you deserved to do so, for the good-will, pluck and courage which you showed."

Light's face beamed with happiness as she spoke these words, for she knew that to deserve to find the Blue Bird was very much the same thing as finding it; but she was not allowed to say this, for it was a beautiful mystery, which Tyltyl had to solve for himself. She turned to the Animals and Things, who stood weeping in a corner, and told them to come and kiss the Children.

Bread at once put down the cage at Tyltyl's feet and be‑gan to make a speech:

"In the name of all, I crave permission . . ."

"You sha'n't have mine!" cried Fire.

"Order!" cried Water.

"We still have tongues of our own!" roared Fire.

"Yes! Yes!" screamed Sugar, who, knowing that his end was at hand, kept kissing Water and melting before the others' eyes.

Poor Bread in vain tried to make his voice heard above the din. Light had to interfere and command silence. Then Bread spoke his last words:

"I am leaving you," he said, between his sobs. "I am leaving you, my dear Children, and you will no longer see me in my living form. . . . Your eyes are about to close to the invisible life of Things; but I shall be always there, in the bread-pan, on the shelf, on the table, beside the soup, I who am, if I may say so, the most faithful companion, the oldest friend of Man. . . ."

"Well, and what about me?" shouted Fire, angrily.

"Silence!" said Light. "The hour is passing. . . . Be quick and say good-bye to the Children. . . ."

Fire rushed forward, took hold of the Children, one after the other, and kissed them so violently that they screamed with pain:

"Oh! Oh! . . . He's burning me! . . ."

"Oh! Oh! . . . He's scorched my nose! . . ."

"Let me kiss the place and make it well," said Water, going up to the children gently.

This gave Fire his chance:

"Take care," he said, "you'll get wet."

"I am loving and gentle," said Water. "I am kind to human beings. . . ."

"What about those you drown?" asked Fire.

But Water pretended not to hear:

"Love the wells, listen to the brooks," she said. "I shall always be there. When you sit down in the evening, beside the springs, try to understand what they are trying to say. . . ."

Then she had to break off, for a regular waterfall of tears came gushing from her eyes, flooding all around her. However, she resumed:

"Think of me when you see the water-bottle. . . . You will find me also in the ewer, the watering-can, the cistern and the tap. . . ."

Then Sugar came up, with a limping walk, for he could hardly stand on his feet. He uttered a few words of sorrow, in an affected voice and then stopped, for tears, he said, were not in harmony with his temperament.

"Humbug!" cried Bread.

"Sugar-plum! Lollipop! Caramel!" yelped Fire.

And all began to laugh, except the two children, who were very sad:

"Where are Tylette and Tylô gone to?" asked our hero.

At that moment, the Cat came running up, in a terrible state: her hair was on end and dishevelled, her clothes were torn and she was holding a handkerchief to her cheek, as though she had the tooth-ache. She uttered terrible groans and was closely pursued by the Dog, who overwhelmed her with bites, blows and kicks. The others rushed in between them to separate them, but the two enemies continued to insult and glare at each other. The Cat accused the Dog of pulling her tail and putting tin tacks in her food and beating her. The Dog simply growled and denied none of his actions:

"You've had some," he kept saying, "you've had some and you're going to have some more!"

But, suddenly, he stopped and, as he was panting with excitement, it could be seen that his tongue turned quite white: Light had told him to kiss the Children for the last time.

"For the last time?" stammered poor Tylô. "Are we to part from these poor Children?"

His grief was such that he was incapable of understanding anything.

"Yes," said Light. "The hour which you know of is at hand. . . . We are going to return to silence. . . ."

Thereupon the Dog, suddenly realizing his misfortune, began to utter real howls of despair and fling himself upon the Children, whom he loaded with mad and violent caresses:

"No! No!" he cried. "I refuse! . . . I refuse! . . . I shall always talk! . . . And I shall be very good. . . . You will keep me with you and I shall learn to read and write and play dominoes! . . . And I shall always be very clean. . . . And I shall never steal anything in the kitchen again. . . ."

He went on his knees before the two Children, sobbing and entreating, and, when Tyltyl, with his eyes full of tears, remained silent, dear Tylô had a last magnificent idea: running up to the Cat, he offered, with smiles that looked like grins, to kiss her. Tylette, who did not possess his spirit of self-sacrifice, leapt back and took refuge by Mytyl's side. Then Mytyl said, innocently:

"You, Tylette, are the only one that hasn't kissed us yet."

The Cat put on a mincing tone:

"Children," said she, "I love you both as much as you deserve."

There was a pause.

"And now," said Light, "let me, in my turn, give you a last kiss. . . ."

As she spoke, she spread her veil round them as if she would have wrapped them for the last time in her luminous might. Then she gave them each a long and loving kiss. Tyltyl and Mytyl hung on to her beseechingly:

"No, no, no, Light!" they cried. "Stay here with us! . . . Daddy won't mind. . . . We will tell Mummy how kind you have been. . . . Where will you go all alone? . . .

"Not very far, my Children," said Light. "Over there to the Land of the Silence of Things."

"No, no," said Tyltyl. "I won't have you go. . . ."

But Light quieted them with a motherly gesture and said words to them which they never forgot. Long after, when they were a grandfather and grandmother in their turn, Tyltyl and Mytyl still remembered them and used to repeat them to their grandchildren.

Here are Light's touching words:

"Listen, Tyltyl. Do not forget, child, that everything that you see in this world has neither beginning nor end. If you keep this thought in your heart and let it grow up with you, you will always, in all circumstances, know what to say, what to do and what to hope for."

And, when our two friends began to sob, she added, lov-ingly:

"Do not cry, my dear little ones. . . . I have not a voice like Water; I have only my brightness, which Man does not understand. . . . But I watch over him to the end of his days. . . . Never forget that I am speaking to you in every spreading moonbeam, in every twinkling star, in every dawn that rises, in every lamp that is lit, in every good and bright thought of your soul. . . ."

At that moment, the grandfather's clock in the cottage struck eight o'clock.   Light stopped for a moment and then, in a voice that grew suddenly fainter, whispered:

"Good-bye! . . . Good-bye! . . . The hour is striking! . . . Good-bye!"

Her veil faded away, her smile became paler, her eyes closed, her form vanished and, through their tears, the chil-dren saw nothing but a thin ray of light dying away at their feet.   Then they turned to the others. . . . but these had disappeared. . . .

The Awakening

CHAPTER X

THE AWAKENING

THE grandfather's clock in Tyl the woodcutter's cottage had struck eight; and his two little Children, Tyltyl and Mytyl, were still asleep in their little beds. Mummy Tyl stood looking at them, with her arms akimbo and her apron tucked up, laughing and scolding in the same breath:

"I can't let them go on sleeping till mid-day," she said. "Come, get up, you little lazybones!"

But it was no use shaking them, kissing them or pulling the bed-clothes off them: they kept on falling back upon their pillows, with their noses pointing at the ceiling, their mouths wide open, their eyes shut and their cheeks all pink.

At last, after receiving a gentle thump in the ribs, Tyltyl opened one eye and murmured:

"What? . . . Light? . . . Where are you? . . . No, no, don't go away. . . ."

"Light!" cried Mummy Tyl, laughing. "Why, of course, it's light. . . . Has been for ever so long! . . . What's the matter with you? . . . You look quite blinded. . . ."

"Mummy! . . . Mummy!" said Tyltyl, rubbing his eyes.
"It's you! . . ."

"Why, of course, it's I! . . . Why do you stare at me
in that way? . . . Is my nose turned upside down, by any
chance?"

Tyltyl was quite awake by this time and did not trouble
to answer the question. He was beside himself with delight! It was ages and ages since he had seen his Mummy
and he never tired of kissing her.

Mummy Tyl began to be uneasy. What could the matter be? Had her boy lost his senses? Here he was suddenly talking of a long journey in the company of the Fairy
and Water and Milk and Sugar and Fire and Bread and
Light! He made believe that he had been away a
year! . . .

"But you haven't left the room!" cried Mummy Tyl,
who was now nearly beside herself with fright. "I put you
to bed last night and here you are this morning! It's
Christmas Day: don't you hear the bells in the village? . . ."

"Of course, it's Christmas Day," said Tyltyl, obstinately,
"seeing that I went away a year ago, on Christmas Eve!
. . . You're not angry with me? . . . Did you feel very
sad? . . . And what did Daddy say? . . ."

"Come, you're still asleep!" said Mummy Tyl, trying to take comfort. "You've been dreaming! . . . Get up and put on your breeches and your little jacket. . . ."

"Hullo, I've got my shirt on!" said Tyltyl.

And, leaping up, he knelt down on the bed and began to dress, while his mother kept on looking at him with a scared face.

The little boy rattled on:

"Ask Mytyl, if you don't believe me. . . . Oh, we have had such adventures! . . . We saw Grandad and Granny . . . yes, in the Land of Memory . . . it was on our way. They are dead, but they are quite well, aren't they, Mytyl?"

And Mytyl, who was now beginning to wake up, joined her brother in describing their visit to the grand-parents and the fun which they had had with their little brothers and sisters.

This was too much for Mummy Tyl. She ran to the door of the cottage and called with all her might to her husband, who was working on the edge of the forest:

"Oh, dear, oh, dear!" she cried. "I shall lose them as I lost the others! . . . Do come! . . . Come quick. . . ."

Daddy Tyl soon entered the cottage, with his axe in his hand; he listened to his wife's lamentations, while the two

Children told the story of their adventures over again and asked him what he had done during the year.

"You see, you see!" said Mummy Tyl, crying. "They have lost their heads, something will happen to them; run and fetch the doctor. . . ."

But the woodcutter was not the man to put himself out for such a trifle. He kissed the little ones, calmly lit his pipe and declared that they looked very well and that there was no hurry.

At that moment, there came a knock at the door and the neighbour walked in. She was a little old woman leaning on a stick and very much like the Fairy Bérylune. The Children at once flung their arms around her neck and capered round her, shouting merrily:

"It's the Fairy Bérylune!"

The neighbour, who was a little hard of hearing, paid no attention to their cries and said to Mummy Tyl:

"I have come to ask for a bit of fire for my Christmas stew. . . . It's very chilly this morning. . . . Good-morning, children. . . ."

Meanwhile, Tyltyl had become a little thoughtful. No doubt, he was glad to see the old Fairy again; but what would she say when she heard that he had not the Blue

Bird? He made up his mind like a man and went up to her boldly:

"Fairy Bérylune, I could not find the Blue Bird. . . ."

"What is he saying?" asked the neighbour, quite taken aback.

Thereupon Mummy Tyl began to fret again:

"Come, Tyltyl, don't you know Goody Berlingot?"

"Why, yes, of course," said Tyltyl, looking the neighbour up and down. "It's the Fairy Bérylune."

"Béry . . . what?" asked the neighbour.

"Bérylune," answered Tyltyl, calmly.

"Berlingot," said the neighbour. "You mean Berlingot."

Tyltyl was a little put out by her positive way of talking; and he answered:

"Bérylune or Berlingot, as you please, ma'am, but I know what I'm saying. . . ."

Daddy Tyl was beginning to have enough of it:

"We must put a stop to this," he said. "I will give them a smack or two."

"Don't," said the neighbour; "it's not worth while. It's only a little fit of dreaming; they must have been sleeping in the moonbeams. . . . My little girl, who is very ill, is often like that. . . ."

Mummy Tyl put aside her own anxiety for a moment and asked after the health of Neighbour Berlingot's little girl.

"She's only so-so," said the neighbour, shaking her head. "She can't get up. . . . The doctor says it's her nerves. . . . I know what would cure her, for all that. She was asking me for it only this morning, for her Christmas present. . . ."

She hesitated a little, looked at Tyltyl with a sigh and added, in a disheartened tone:

"What can I do? It's a fancy she has. . . ."

The others looked at one another in silence: they knew what the neighbour's words meant. Her little girl had long been saying that she would get well if Tyltyl would only give her his dove; but he was so fond of it that he refused to part with it. . . .

"Well," said Mummy Tyl to her son, "won't you give your bird to that poor little thing? She has been dying to have it for ever so long! . . ."

"My bird!" cried Tyltyl, slapping his forehead as though they had spoken of something quite out of the way. "My bird!" he repeated. "That's true, I was forgetting about him! . . . And the cage! . . . Mytyl, do you see the cage? . . . It's the one which Bread carried. . . . Yes, yes, it's the same one, there it is, there it is!"

Tyltyl would not believe his eyes. He took a chair, put it under the cage and climbed on to it gaily, saying:

"Of course, I'll give him to her, of course, I will! . . ."

Then he stopped, in amazement:

"Why, he's blue!" he said. "It's my dove, just the same, but he has turned blue while I was away!"

And our hero jumped down from the chair and began to skip for joy, crying:

"It's the Blue Bird we were looking for! We have been miles and miles and miles and he was here all the time! . . . He was here, at home! . . . Oh, but how wonderful! . . . Mytyl, do you see the bird? What would Light say? . . . There, Madame Berlingot, take him quickly to your little girl. . . ."

While he was talking, Mummy Tyl threw herself into her husband's arms and moaned:

"You see? . . . You see? . . . He's taken bad again. . . . He's wandering. . . ."

Meantime, Neighbour Berlingot beamed all over her face, clasped her hands together and mumbled her thanks. When Tyltyl gave her the bird, she could hardly believe her eyes. She hugged the boy in her arms and wept with joy and gratitude:

"Do you give it me?" she kept saying. "Do you give

it me like that, straight away and for nothing? . . . Good‧
ness, how happy she will be! . . . I fly, I fly! . . . I will
come back to tell you what she says. . . ."

"Yes, yes, go quickly," said Tyltyl, "for some of them
change their colour!"

Neighbour Berlingot ran out and Tyltyl shut the door
after her. Then he turned round on the threshold, looked
at the walls of the cottage, looked all around him and
seemed wonderstruck:

"Daddy, Mummy, what have you done to the house?"
he asked. "It's just as it was, but it's much prettier."

His parents looked at each other in bewilderment; and the
little boy went on:

"Why, yes, everything has been painted and made to
look like new; everything is clean and polished. . . . And
look at the forest outside the window! . . . How big and
fine it is! . . . One would think it was quite new! . . .
How happy I feel here, oh, how happy I feel!"

The worthy woodcutter and his wife could not make out
what was coming over their son; but you, my dear little
readers, who have followed Tyltyl and Mytyl through their
beautiful dream, will have guessed what it was that altered
everything in our young hero's view.

It was not for nothing that the Fairy, in his dream, had

given him a talisman to open his eyes. He had learnt to
see the beauty of things around him; he had passed through
trials that had developed his courage; while pursuing the
Blue Bird, the Bird of Happiness that was to bring happiness to the Fairy's little girl, he had become open-handed
and so good-natured that the mere thought of giving pleasure to others filled his heart with joy. And, while trav-
elling through endless, wonderful, imaginary regions, his
mind had opened out to life.

The boy was right, when he thought everything more
beautiful, for, to his richer and purer understanding, everything must needs seem infinitely fairer than before.

Meanwhile, Tyltyl continued his joyful inspection of
the cottage. He leant over the bread-pan to speak a kind
word to the Loaves; he rushed at Tylô, who was sleeping in
his basket, and congratulated him on the good fight which
he had made in the forest.

Mytyl stooped down to stroke Tylette, who was snoozing
by the stove, and said:

"Well, Tylette? . . . You know me, I see, but you
have stopped talking."

Then Tyltyl put his hand up to his forehead:

"Hullo!" he cried. "The diamond's gone! . . . Who's
taken my little green hat? . . . Never mind, I don't want

it any more! . . . Ah, there's Fire! Good-morning, sir!
He'll be crackling to make Water angry!" He ran to the
tap, turned it on and bent down over the water. "Good-
morning, Water, good-morning! . . . What does she
say? . . . She still talks, but I don't understand her as
well as I did. . . . Oh, how happy I am, how happy I
am! . . ."

"So am I, so am I!" cried Mytyl.

And our two young friends took each other's hands and
began to scamper round the kitchen.

Mummy Tyl felt a little relieved at seeing them so full
of life and spirits. Besides, Daddy Tyl was so calm and
placid. He sat eating his porridge and laughing:

"You see, they are *playing* at being happy!" he said.

Of course, the poor dear man did not know that a wonderful dream had taught his little children not to play at
being happy, but to *be* happy, which is the greatest and most
difficult of lessons.

"I like Light best of all," said Tyltyl to Mytyl, standing
on tip-toe by the window. "You can see her over there,
through the trees of the forest. To-night, she will be in the
lamp. Dear, oh, dear, how lovely it all is and how glad I
feel, how glad I . . ."

He stopped and listened. Everybody lent an ear. They

heard laughter and merry voices; and the sounds came nearer.

"It's her voice!" cried Tyltyl. "Let me open the door!"

As a matter of fact, it was the little girl, with her mother, Neighbour Berlingot.

"Look at her," said Goody Berlingot, quite overcome with joy. "She can run, she can dance, she can fly! It's a miracle! When she saw the bird, she jumped, just like that. . . ."

And Goody Berlingot hopped from one leg to the other at the risk of falling and breaking her long, hooked nose.

The Children clapped their hands and everybody laughed.

The little girl was there, in her long white night-dress, standing in the middle of the kitchen, a little surprised to find herself on her feet after so many months' illness. She smiled and pressed Tyltyl's dove to her heart.

Tyltyl looked first at the child and then at Mytyl:

"Don't you think she's very like Light?" he asked.

"She is much smaller," said Mytyl.

"Yes, indeed!" said Tyltyl. "But she will grow! . . ."

And the three Children tried to put a little food down the Bird's beak, while the parents began to feel easier in their minds and looked at them and smiled.

Tyltyl was radiant. I will not conceal from you, my dear little readers, that the Dove had hardly changed colour at all and that it was joy and happiness that decked him with a magnificent bright blue plumage in our hero's eyes. No matter! Tyltyl, without knowing it, had discovered Light's great secret, which is *that we draw nearer to happiness by trying to give it to others.*

But now something happened. Everybody became excited, the Children screamed, the parents threw up their arms and rushed to the open door: the Bird had suddenly escaped! He was flying away as fast as he could.

"My bird! My bird!" sobbed the little girl.

But Tyltyl was the first to run to the staircase and he returned in triumph:

"It's all right!" he said. "Don't cry! He is still in the house and we shall find him again."

And he gave a kiss to the little girl, who was already smiling through her tears:

"You'll be sure to catch him again, won't you?" she asked.

"Trust me," replied our friend, confidentially. "I now know where he is."

You also, my dear little readers, now know where the

Blue Bird is. Dear Light revealed nothing to the wood-cutter's Children, but she showed them the road to happiness by teaching them to be good and kind and generous.

Suppose that, at the beginning of this story, she had said to them:

"Go straight back home. The Blue Bird is there, in the humble cottage, in the wicker cage, with your dear father and mother who love you."

The Children would never have believed her:

"What!" Tyltyl would have answered. "The Blue Bird, my dove? Nonsense: my dove is grey! . . . Happiness, in the cottage? With Daddy and Mummy? Oh, I say! There are no toys at home and it's awfully boring there: we want to go ever so far and meet with tremendous adventures and have all sorts of fun. . . ."

That is what he would have said; and he and Mytyl would have set out in spite of everything, without listening to Light's advice, for the most certain truths are good for nothing if we do not put them to the test ourselves. It only takes a moment to tell a child all the wisdom in the world, but our whole lives are not long enough to help us understand it, because our own experience is our only light.

Each of us must seek out happiness for himself; and he

has to take endless pains and undergo many a cruel disappointment before he learns to become happy by appreciating the simple and perfect pleasures that are always within easy reach of his mind and heart.

THE END

CPSIA information can be obtained
at www.ICGtesting.com
Printed in the USA
BVHW041746100319
542262BV00007B/30/P

—